To my nephew Nasir; with love; remembering your love and concern ._. Let us listen Together. God bless you —

Azar 6.2.7.06

Listening To Jesus

God's miracles in the life of a Christian minister preaching in the Middle East.

by
Najeeb Azar

Bloomington, IN Milton Keynes, UK

authorHOUSE

AuthorHouse™
1663 Liberty Drive, Suite 200
Bloomington, IN 47403
www.authorhouse.com
Phone: 1-800-839-8640

AuthorHouse™ UK Ltd.
500 Avebury Boulevard
Central Milton Keynes, MK9 2BE
www.authorhouse.co.uk
Phone: 08001974150

This book is a work of non-fiction. Unless otherwise noted, the author and the publisher make no explicit guarantees as to the accuracy of the information contained in this book and in some cases, names of people and places have been altered to protect their privacy.

First published by AuthorHouse 5/31/2006

ISBN: 1-4259-1713-5 (sc)

Library of Congress Control Number: 2006903072

Printed in the United States of America
Bloomington, Indiana
This book is printed on acid-free paper.

Dedication

I dedicate this book to my beloved wife Najla who stood by me all those years to help, support and remind me of all that happened that was recorded in this book. She hoped it would be published in her lifetime. She was my best friend and helper in all times hard and easy and was the best mother ever. I loved and will still love her forever.

To my son Victor for his hard labor in editing and getting this book set in the right form to read and be understood.

Special thanks to Ron Bartrons for his friendship and encouragement.

I dedicate this book to my Children Viola, Katy and Samir who encouraged me and made life easy for me to produce this work.

I would also like to acknowledge all my grand children. I like to acknowledge especially Angie whom I consider the family's artist and photographer who produced the art for the front and the back of this book as well as redoing the two charts on Love and Faith.

After reading this book, you will enroll and join the followers of the prince of peace in promoting and spreading peace, love and unity, so we can enjoy living in a new safe and happy world.

Contents

Introduction

In the Middle East, I was a minister with the Seventh day Adventist Church for 32 years. I did my best to promote that churches' doctrines, went through so many hardships, persecutions, and having being suspected of being connected with the Jews because we kept Saturday for a Sabbath. Now, I am still a Christian and I follow Jesus' commandments of love on which hang all the prophets and the old laws. As I read the Bible more and more, I found that I understood it differently before. The Bible tells in Dan. 12:4 that knowledge increases in the last days of this earth's history. Again, reading Duet. 5:15, it tells very plainly that God gave the Sabbath to the Jews as a sign of delivering them from the Egyptian bondage. The apostle Paul mentions in Gal. 4:10 that Christians should not keep those days and festivals kept in the Old Testament. He is afraid that if they did, he would have labored for them in vain. He also warns against those who condemn each other for keeping a different day than the day they keep, that it is up to the individual to choose the day to worship his God on as it is in 1Cor. 6:12 & 13, and Gal. 4:10 & 11 and Rom. 14:5. He goes further to tell us in Heb. 4:7 & 8 that the Jews never kept that day or the Sabbath in the way that God wanted them to keep it. Isaiah was disgusted by the way that they worshiped God, that he told them speaking for God in Isa. 1:13 & 14, that God is no more interested in their offerings and Sabbaths, he would not honor them. In Heb. 4:7 & 8, God says through the apostle Paul that He introduced another Sabbath for his followers, namely the day you receive Jesus as your personal savior.

So why be so much tied to days and months and be distracted from the main important issue which is Jesus Christ. Paul wants us to stop arguing and condemning each other concerning days, eating and drinking and live the Christian life.

This book is about God's miracles in my life and in my family's life in the Middle East. It is also a testament of God's Love and power, which had saved and protected us through many wars and dangerous times. Through this book, you will also get a glimpse of what it is like to be Christians in the Middle East. You will also experience through the many stories how Moslems view Christians and Christianity. Many of your preconceptions and stereotypes will be shattered. Perhaps you will start to understand the complex nature of this area. After you read the book, you will start seeing the world from a different point of view and the current news in the popular media will become more interesting.

A Goat For A Nursing Mother

I was born to my father and mother as the second son, on June 19, 1920. My Father's name was Naser Azar. Naser Azar's family produced nine children, five daughters and four sons. I was the second of four sons.

The day I was born was a great day for my family. A big celebration was organized and all of the close relatives were invited. My father was ecstatic that his second boy had arrived. Growing up as a boy in a Christian home was a blessing. In the Middle East, baby boys were more desirable than baby girls. So parents are usually happier when boys are born. Their reasoning is that a boy carries his father's name and will help his father earn a living for the family. Young boys accompany their fathers to the fields to plant, harvest or tend to the sheep. Girls were thought not to have economical value because they will end up benefiting their husband's families. This culture did not make for an ideal ground for women or their rights. During that time, women accepted their role and lived in harmony with their environment.

To illustrate the disparity in how this issue was viewed. I would like to share the story of how my father was born and circumstances that surrounded his birth. My father had been the fifteenth child born to his father and was the only baby boy, following 14 daughters born before him. It shook his mother to learn from the midwife that he was a baby boy, she died right away, within minutes. It is said she was noticeably happy, without ever having seen her son, that she had finally produced a boy for her family.

As a baby, my father was shown much mercy and love from other women who already had children, as they shared the milk their bodies

1

had produced for their own babies, with the fifteenth child born to the dead woman. One of those compassionate and kind women happened to be his oldest sister, a mother, laden with milk for her new baby and her new brother.

His sister played the part of his missing mother, but God miraculously provided another means. It was in fact considered a miracle by the local folk. With no lead, and no direction that anyone could see, one of the female goats that belonged to the family would come into the baby's room once a day. She would stand over the new baby boy.

She would place her udder over his cradle in such a way that it was possible for him to feed on her milk. We do not know the name of the dear and miraculous goat, but the baby, my father, was named Naser, which means "victor". The goat continued to come until Naser was naturally weaned, and ready to eat solid food.

The Sea Of Galilee

Another great day for our family was the day when my father's three older sons, four more candidates and two Pastors made their way in a bus to the Jordan River for baptism. It was on June 11, 1937. The baptism took place in the traditional spot, a place considered by all to be the location where our savior Jesus Christ was baptized. The Jordan River is a desired place for Christians to be baptized in the Middle East. When they reached the river, they found that the water was very high and dangerous.

We all knew that whenever it flowed as swiftly as it was, the water became muddy. It was written in the Old Testament that the muddy water was the reason for Naaman the Syrian not to want to dip himself in its waters. He was ordered by the prophet Elisha (2 Kings 5:10) to dip himself seven times to be healed from his leprosy. He declined to dip himself even once of the seven times. Naaman said he would rather be dipped in one of Syria's other two great rivers instead - namely Abana, which is now called Barada, the river that runs through the city of Damascus. And Farfar, the second river, now called Al-Awaj, originates from Jabal Ash-Shaikh (mount Hermon). These two rivers were and still are both clear and clean.

You would think that a leper, in order to be healed from his leprosy, would accept any kind of water, even the most dirty of water for a moment, in order to be healed. Naaman was convinced to go into and through the Jordan River. He left me a good example to follow. If I was seeking healing from whatever disease I would be confronted with I would just go through the water.

Finding out we should not have the baptism in the Jordan, because it was so dangerous was truly disappointing. We headed towards the Sea of Galilee. It had some wonderful memories connected with it also, and it was not as treacherous.

On the northern end of the Sea of Galilee lay Capernaum, which the Lord Jesus took as His home. It was here that He taught and performed many of His miracles. Here He commanded the storm to stop. And on its banks He appeared to His Followers after His resurrection.

The seven candidates and myself went into the water both to die and be reborn with our Savior. It was a great inspirational day. My father was watching from the shore. He was overwhelmed with happiness.

I remarked later, that "Yes, he wanted to see his children follow in both his and his Master's steps. Naser's Baptism took place in 1929 with a group of believers from his family - The Azars. My father was happy and grateful to be the first to be baptized in the North of Jordan. He and that group founded the first Seventh Day Adventist church in that area.

But as I was going into the watery grave this time. With the right hand over his candidate the Pastor asked "Brother Najeeb, why do you want to be baptized?" I said that I needed to be baptized so that I may belong to Jesus. He left me an example, which he expects me to follow, and I don't want to disappoint Him. I want my sins forgiven. I want Him and need him to uphold me from now on whenever I fall."

After the baptism, pastor Bethman looked at me and said, "Do you expect any other help Najeeb, such as an education?" "Not now, not yet," was my positive reply. I was wrong, as young men can often be wrong, and answered too quickly. That question and answer made it very hard for me two years later.

I was offered the opportunity to enter Middle East College (a Seventh Day Adventist College, located in Beirut, Lebanon.) Even though the education fees at that time (1939) did not exceed the equivalent of $35 US dollars for tuition, room and board put together, I could not afford to pay even that small sum.

In the summer of 1938, one year after my baptism I was called to spend three months with Pastor Bethman, who had baptized me. He lived and preached in Amman, the capital of Jordan. Back then it used to be a couple of hours bus ride to travel from my hometown of Al-Husn south to Amman. Pastor Bethman wanted to mentor and prepare me for preaching. At that time, like all other times in history, we used to believe that the "end," (literally the End of time, and the coming of Christ) was very near, and wanted to have as many of the Children of God as possible united, working as a combined effort within the evangelistic force. I happened to be one of those who had been chosen from my childhood to do the Lord's work. My schoolmates called me Pastor even while I was yet a child.

Pastor Bethman would ask me to sit representing an audience, and he would preach a sermon. The next day the Pastor would sit down and listen in turn to his student preaching the same sermon. Those were precious days. I was both criticized and commended. That was the beginning of God's call to me to join the ministry.

My Father's Death

July 31, 1939 was an awful day. It was never expected that my father should die then. He was young, only in his sixties. His father (my grand father lived well beyond 100 and was not sick not even one day of his life.) Many others and myself looked upon his death as untimely, a mistake of Gods'. But how could we lift our voices or eyes upward and speak judgment on Gods' choice or to question what he does?

That death left me with the responsibility of a large family without an income, excluding the few sheep we raised for milk, and some wheat which was produced in our field, which we used for the making of bread.

Among those who came to comfort us was the bishop of the Anglican Church accompanied by his parish board members. My father had belonged to that church prior to becoming a Seventh Day Adventist. The bishop had been told of our very difficult situation and wanted to help us. On the other hand they had never been pleased that my father had joined another church, in an entirely different Christian denomination.

The bishop began talking to my mother making a very generous offer. There was no question that it was not motivated by love.

"My dear uncles' wife, he started (He was my fathers nephew.) We are very sad it has turned out this way. We understand how you feel, and would like to be of help. Words alone cannot console, therefore, as a family we are proposing a plan that we offer to you as members of our family."

My mother asked what plan that might be, and the Bishop said, "We want to send Najeeb to London, England to study theology and

6

in the future become a Pastor in his Father's original church. And we want to assure you that we as a church family will take care of you all, as family, and help you financially until you can stand on your own feet. What answer do you have for such an offer?"

Who or what church would make such an offer? Surely they were bereaved members of our family as well. They spoke the words and then acted out their words with deeds. Who would offer such generous help?

My mother referred the bishop to me for an answer. Either we accept and enjoy our people's love and care, or reject it and be alone. That visit was made before any of our own Mission officials even had it in mind to make the obligatory comfort-call on us. "Yes, dear bishop," I answered, "We appreciate your very warm and generous offer. It is one which is rarely found anywhere in the world nowadays. And we will come back to my Father's original church. Would you mind however, if I had only one condition?" My uncle, the Bishop of the Anglican Church, asked me what that condition might be.

"Allow me to keep Saturday for my Sabbath?"

"My answer is no. We want to get rid of the Saturday of the Jews and free you from those limitations of the letter of the Law. We want to put an end to the new church your Father brought to the North of Jordan. What do you say? We want you and we will help you".

"I agree to that also, but again there is one condition."

"What is it son?"

"If you can prove to me that Saturday is not biblical and that Sunday is the Lord's Day, I will do as you ask."

It took a few moments. Both parties had to think about it. This was an important, sincere and generous offer! Should we turn it down? Could we accept it, and live, honestly before the Lord? Then the bishop looked up to me and said, "Najeeb, my dear son, I cannot prove it to you from the Bible. You are sincere and honest in what you believe. Though I believe that you are wrong. Najeeb, you will have to stay where you are and God bless you." There were tears in some eyes and a few respectful smiles on some other faces.

My folks and myself stayed where we were. I did not go to London, England. I stayed where I was and God, in all of His Mercy has very richly blessed that decision. All Praise to God. That bishop was never against us, and he remained one of our very best friends. All thanks to our Good Lord!

August 1939, one month after my Father's death, the Pastor of our own church came to see us and to bring us comfort. Our Pastors were always too busy to visit and we were accustomed to their excuses. We loved and admired our pastor. All of our church members respected and loved those that they considered their spiritual leaders.

On his visit, the Pastor offered me the opportunity to join Middle East College in Beirut, Lebanon. "Pastor," I said, "Thank you very much for the offer, but I cannot accept it."

"Why brother Najeeb"?

"I have no means with which to pay for my education."

"Never mind that, God will take care of you."

"What about my mother, my sisters and my brothers. Am I to do this instead of finding a job to help take care of them? Is it good to leave them?"

"God will take care of them too. You must prepare for the ministry. This is God's call for you."

My younger brother had to join the army in order to help the family financially. And I joined Middle East College, with one cheap suit, to suit all occasions. God and hard work on my part took care of my education. They both served to start me on His service. How glad and grateful I was and still am for His goodness and grace!

I spent three years at Middle East College. I graduated with good grades. I completed the curriculum. My degree and that graduation carry no weight now. But are still a fond memory of a gift from God, and my discipline to see it through.

There were twelve of us in that first class, in that first year of the college. We referred to ourselves as the twelve apostles.

Starting My Ministry In 1940

The late elder, pastor Keough, an Irishman was in charge of the mission work then. During two of those summers he gave me work to do. He told me to go preaching from door to door.

"How could I do it?" I asked, I have very little knowledge in preaching?"

"You will visit the families with your Bible. They will let you in. Greet them and tell them you want to read for them from the Holy Book. They will be happy to hear it. Read one chapter, and explain simply what you have read. Answer their questions as best as you can. Conclude your visit with a prayer. Never, ever leave a home without praying."

He helped me make a daily schedule, which I followed. Holding two to three cottage meetings a night. This work ended when Elder Keough visited me one day in the summer of 1940. He had brought three bolts of cloth with him, which he gave me. He wanted me to have the cloth made into three suits for myself. It was a great gesture from a non-Arab man following our Lord Jesus, in the Middle East.

I began my ministry in 1942. I had already graduated from the Middle East College. I was a young man. I had many wonderful "young man" dreams that were soon to be transformed into the realities offered up by the world. There was the preparation for the great work to be done. That summer I covered the whole area with visitation.

Many people, whole families started coming to church to watch the young Pastor preaching. We were not content with little results. Our Good God could give us the best. Villages all around were reached out with the seeds of the ever-present truth of God, and the Adventist way.

That resulted in much opposition directed towards the work. I cannot say that opposition was not expected. Hadn't Jesus known that there would be adversity and wasn't he ready to meet it as it came?

Well my dear reader, if you have ever followed your Savior, and have worked to show His love to those who walk in darkness, surely the prince of darkness will oppose the light you bring to illuminate his wickedness. Those who continue entertaining the deeds of the dark world will, most assuredly, oppose those who love the light and begin to walk in it.

The work in North Jordan was going forward. It was becoming successful. One afternoon I received a cable from the Missions Head office, in Beirut, Lebanon with the words:

"Proceed immediately to Karak"

That cable did not make me happy. I considered the work I was doing mine, and that I should be left there until I could harvest those souls I had been preparing for the Kingdom. I wanted also to organize a church. Often the Lords' thought's and plans differ completely from ours.

The biblical name for Karak is Moab. The name comes, from Moab the son of Lot, from one of his two daughters. The Moabites are the descendants of one of Lot's sons (Gen. 19: 30-38.) It was here that Ruth the Moabite lived with her mother in law after the death of her husband. This is the Land of Ruth who became the great, great grandmother of our Savior. As the cable came all of these thoughts came rushing through my imagination, and I wondered if there was another Ruth there, a woman or even a man, ready to accept the Savior in that great and ancient city!

There was a man. His name was Isbir Medanat. He is the descendant of Abraham through Ketourah his wife whom he married after Sarah died (Gen. 25:12), The third son Keturah bore for Abraham was called Medan, the father of the Medanat tribe. the Medanat family is very large and they still live in Karak to this day.

This man read his Bible every day. He discovered as a result of his dedication, fasting, and prayer as well as through visions that God wanted him to keep Saturday as His Sabbath. He began keeping it twenty years before he ever knew there were any people in the world, other than the Jews observing the Sabbath on Saturdays. It was a deliberate act of his conscience, reacting to his conviction of that truth in the Holy Word.

When he heard that there were some people already observing the Saturday Sabbath, and that they were Christians somewhere in Jordan, he wrote asking that a preacher be sent to him to help him know his Bible better. That was the basis or cause of the mission presidency sending that cable to me.

What I saw as a poorly rendered, bureaucratic decision was in fact a blessing from the God that I served, a blessing for Mr. Isbir Medanath, and myself. I was on my way to Karak the next day, definitely one of the advantages of being single and ready to move at any moment.

I held the first evangelistic meeting, the very night I reached Karak, even before seeing Isbir. He lived 25 miles west of the city. I either had to go down to the Jordan valley to see him and share Gods confirming word with him, or he had to come up to Karak to me. He lived by the Dead Sea, where he had his land and house.

Yes, I was on my way to visit him the next day.

The Angels Revealed My Identity Before Hand.

I could not understand in the beginning why he was so happy to see me coming to him, until after reading the first text that I chose from the Bible, then he stopped me from proceeding saying, "May I interrupt please?"

"Certainly, what is on your mind?"

He showed me that he had written in a book, the descriptions *given* to him by an angel that preceding night. It was stated about the preacher who was sent to him, and the scriptures that preacher would read as he would start his Bible study.

"You see, he said, you are the man sent for me by the angel."

I began studying with him and his family. The studies continued for two months. Shortly thereafter they all were baptized. Visitation was my next concern. Every body should be reached with the message. Many enrolled in the Bible course by correspondence.

Visitation on foot was necessary for those living in remote villages. Vehicles were never accessible any time you needed them. Also, it would involve much money, which we did not have. The budget was too little in proportion with the goals we had set for ourselves to reach. The head office scheduled us and gave us very limited amount to spend.

Witnessing On Foot From Town to Town

One of those visits was scheduled on a winter day. I was hoping it would not be a rainy one because we would be walking. Another minister accompanied me. We started from Karak walking down the mountain to climb another mountain. The weather was good and the sky was clear as we started that afternoon. The valley we were going through surrounded Karak from all directions, Karak itself being a city built on top of a high mountain with an old fortress built long ago. The ruins of that fortress testify to the city's great regional importance in old times.

One of those events that took place in Moab is recorded in Numbers 22-24. That's when Balak sent for Balaam to curse Israel. His expected curse turned out to be a blessing at that time. When you are with the Lord, He will turn all curses into blessings for you.

As we began to get to the bottom of that mountain, and started the climb up the opposite side, the weather changed and rain began coming down heavily. We got very wet, but had to continue.

A group of interested people was waiting for us at the village of Addar. They had built a fire and were ready to warm and dry the visiting missionaries. As we entered their home they were happy to meet us. We were given clean, dry clothing and ours were set out to dry.

The meeting was held and some of the people present accepted Jesus as their Savior. Happiness filled that house.

We had some inconveniences that night which made it almost impossible for my fellow minister to sleep. I was personally far to weary to be irritated, and far too sleepy to miss the rest and comfort Gods' gift of sleep.

When we awoke, we found out that it had snowed a great deal during the night. The world outside our uncomfortable little quarters looked beautiful and white. The sun would come up shortly and melt it all away. Middle Eastern people always take advantage whenever it snows, enjoying the sight of and playing with snowballs before it melts. We had to go back to Karak that morning.

As usual there were no cars to be found in Addar that morning, we, had to travel on foot. There would be nothing to hinder us from doing God's work by His power and grace. When these dear villagers saw that we were determined to go on foot, they offered us two of their horses to use. Our long ride on those horses that day was so pleasant. We moved smoothly and silently through that wonderful, white robed hills and mountains.

The plan was to get on the bus to travel to Amman, the capital of Jordan, as soon as we got to Karak. We found out we were a few minutes too late to catch the bus. It travels to Amman every morning. So we were forced to take a taxi instead. We soon heard the news that the bus we had intended to take had a bad accident and some of those passengers were killed.

We were indeed sad for those lost to their loved ones. But we took the taxi ride and what we had earlier seen as a great and expensive inconvenience to be God's wonderful providence, sparing us, so we might live to fulfill our appointed tasks for Him. We praised Him for His love and His abiding care.

That trip to Addar resulted in my coming down with and suffering much from pneumonia, and for several months I had to stay at a hospital. It was a small price to pay for God's providence.

Our Creator's ways are sometimes very strange indeed and beyond our comprehension. There are times that He wants His servants just to sit still, to relax and meditate on Him and Him alone. "Not by strength nor by power but by my Spirit" says the Lord.

While in that hospital. I would not accept the idea of being sick. Some I considered were in a more desperate situation and needed someone to visit them. So I started a work of visitation in Lebanon in that hospital.

It was looked upon as unusual for a sick man to visit other sick men. But it seemed logical to me that other patients would welcome my visits and conversation. They would appreciate being visited by someone who understands their situation and happened to be hospitalized like them. I considered the visitation rounds as important in some aspects as those, being made by the nurses and caregivers trained by the doctors. Many of the people there in the hospital, with their various medical problems needed faith and courage as much as they needed diagnosis and medicines. When I would pray with the sick it was noticeable that it made their sufferings lighter. I have always believed that it actually led them even closer to healing. God's love and concern and the good and faithful will of the diligent care of the doctors and their medicines, will bring healing to the body and the spirit.

Those visits were not limited to those I knew as friends. Everyone who asked for them were included. Some did not like me to visit and to pray for them. They reported their dissatisfaction to the hospital's head office.

The Doctor in charge had a talk with me and asked me about what kind of visitation I was doing. I had a conversation with him about God's work. He said later, "If this man is helping out patients to have faith in God, and as a result might speed up their recovery he is helping me too. No one should ever accuse him for the good work he's doing." The doctor was pleased, and wished me well.

Welfare

The church welfare work in Jordan was hard to do. We used to receive loads of clothing and blankets from aid organizations in the west to be able to distribute them to the poor. It is as hard to determine who was actually in need and then to get them satisfied with what they would receive. To make alterations on clothing and other personal articles would take up the time we were supposed to be using for the visitation work. To call in other local ladies to do the mending was harder still.

I remember on one occasion, a lady came back several times to exchange some of the clothes she had gotten. She said they did not fit her. My Wife could not stand it any longer, so this time, she opened her own closet for that woman, inviting her to pick any piece she desired. That lady became ashamed of her self and went away. We learned later, that she was trading the clothes given by the welfare committee for those considered not as good. She really had a wardrobe of clothes, and was not really in need. She was just taking advantage of the church welfare work.

Some would get those pieces of clothes or blankets which were supposed to warm them in cold times, and sell them. We had to make allowances for such behavior. They might have had enough clothing or bedding. They might have had a need of buying some more important things with the price, of those sold. We did not want to be too hard on these people. This was after all, a charity work, a work of provision and love.

Again it was hard to pick members who would think of the interests of others, to take time to pick the right piece for the right person in a family. We wanted to be as fare as possible to everybody, and would share the work we did with others. People are honored when they participate in the work done for the poor and needy, yet those in need can be hurt when they are given such a great task caring for others that they cannot take care of their own needs as well.

The church is supposed to be a wonderful brotherhood, and those who are rich, should work for the happiness of the needy.

First False Messiah Debunked: 1945

From Lebanon I got a call to go and start work in the Bethlehem district in Palestine. Beitjala is a town in the Bethlehem district. This area is one mile west of Bethlehem and had been chosen for me to start evangelistic work. It was here that I met Dr. Moses who had proclaimed himself as the messiah.

In my preaching I made an effort to point out to those who attended the meeting that Christ the Messiah of the Lord came once and will come again to put an end to sin, suffering and death. That preaching contradicted what Dr. Moses proclaimed.

Twenty years prior to my meeting him, many from different nationalities and religions believed in him. He used to perform many miracles of healing. Moslems, Jews, and Christians joined in welcoming him that year. They mounted him on a white horse and paraded him through the streets of old Jerusalem, shouting Hosanna, blessed is he who comes in the name of the Lord.

He heard of my preaching, and was displeased.

Prior to that time, he asked that we as a mission print for him his messages, which he gave away, approving him as the messiah. That request was not granted.

His messages, which he wrote, always started with the heading, "A message of peace from Shalom, the Prince of Peace to Jerusalem the city of peace." Shalom was the name he gave to himself. Shalom means Peace. He quoted many texts from the Bible in which he referred to himself as the messianic individual being spoken of in the texts.

We met one morning in the Beitjala market place where he lived and which he took to be the original Ephrata (Beitjala's ancient name) from which the messiah is supposed to appear.

"Good morning Mr. Azar" he began.

"Good morning Dr. Moses, How are you?"

"How did you know me?"

"Well, exactly the way you knew me. It is no secret Doctor, we heard about each other and could tell who we were."

"Oh yes, would you like to read my messages Mr. Azar, I'd be happy to send them to you", if you would.

"Is it that important Dr. Moses that I should read them?"

"Yes it is, you would get acquainted with me through those messages."

"Now after reading them, do you want us to meet and discuss them?"

"I'd love to."

"Do you mind Doctor, if others were invited to listen to the discussions?"

"Surely I wouldn't mind that"

The time and place for that meeting were arranged. His messages were read. He'd always sent a copy to the British queen, asking that he be crowned king over Palestine in Jerusalem. We had three sessions with many people attending.

He started the discussion, "Did you read my messages Mr. Azar?"

"Yes I did."

"Surely you believe now that I am the Messiah."

"Well, to be honest, reading those messages made me a firm believer that Jesus Christ, who was, is and will always be the Messiah. He already came once, and is coming again soon, the second time."

"What do you mean?"

"The Holy scriptures foretold that prior to His second coming, false messiahs and false prophets would appear."

"Does this mean I belong to this class of people?" As he said that, he became restless.

"Why should it, I hope you are not. Then what priority do we as people or angels have over any others in the sight of God? Don't you believe doctor, that in every nation there are those who love God and worship Him." Again, Palestinians resided in Palestine long before Abraham entered into it. Were you the one born of the Virgin Mary as prophesied by Isaiah in 7:14? Again are you the one who was crucified, and in what manner did you now return from heaven?"

"Mr. Azar, why don't we go over those scriptures I have designated, from the Old Testament they prove I am the Messiah."

We discussed those prophecies he mentioned which actually proved nothing. Some of them were given on conditional basis, and others did not apply. That ended his claims, at least scripture wise.

Then he turned to another argument. "You know Mr. Azar," he said, "All the Arabs have homes with the exception of the Jews. Don't you think the world should have sympathy towards them and help them have their own State?"

"Why not", I said, "They should have one. However, it seems that your real agenda is the establishment of a home for the Jews. You think that by proclaiming yourself the Messiah, people, including the Palestinians, will accept what you say as the word of God and thus accept giving up Palestine for the Jews to live in"

"Well this is what I am trying to do. Everybody should learn of this important fact, especially the Christian world."

"Now where do you want to locate your people?"

"Here in their own country which was promised by God."

"This land, Palestine, has already got its own inhabitants."

"Right, but it should be given to its rightful owners, the Jews according to God's promises."

"God, dear doctor, gave it to them in the past. As far as future was concerned, that was based on conditions of obedience. And what about Ishmael who was Abraham's son? His descendants claim the land to be theirs as well. It is their right too. God blessed Ishmael for the sake of Abraham (Gen.17:20). Now Ishmael had a Jewish father and an Egyptian mother and Egyptian wife. He is half Jewish and half Egyptian. In fact the Jews and the Moslems are brothers (Gen. 16:12 and 21:21). Why not live together? "

"My people, the Jews, will turn back to God, "The Land that flows with milk and honey will be theirs again."

"I'm afraid that, while you are trying to convince the Jews that they'd find milk and honey, coming over, leaving their present homes and properties, they would discover that there was no milk and no honey compared to what they had formerly."

"But, doesn't it really belong to them?"

"Why don't we leave those residing now in Palestine where they are? Otherwise it would mean sending them out and start admitting only those who are God's true worshipers. Could you be able to know those?"

"Honestly no, I could not."

"You know God alone will separate the good from the bad. This would be accomplished only when Jesus comes back. Then, it will not be only Palestine; but rather He will give the whole earth to those who love Him indeed."

Another False Messiah Saved: 1946

The Mission committee asked me to do some visitation in Jerusalem. Some times the church Pastor left for other assignments out of town, and I had to take over on Sabbath mornings' services in Jerusalem.

Some members knew English. Others understood Arabic only. So I had, having none to translate, to prepare my sermon in both languages. I would talk a portion of the sermon in Arabic, and then tell the same in English, until the sermon was over.

At that time I wanted to draw a picture expressing my love for my Savior. As I was working on that piece, a young, German woman used to visit me. She loved me extremely and wanted to insure similar love from me. In Jordan you cannot date a girl unless you plan to marry her. To go out with a girl and later leave her out is considered a reproach and that lady would be looked down upon. The subject of marriage was a negative concept to me, even though I was 26 Years old. When she saw that I was deaf to her pleadings and stubborn in my resolve, she left me alone. Thank God. She used to remark "You are in love with your God, and Him only." As this was the only piece for "love" that I was making. His banner over me is love (chart)

More and more antichrists appeared during those two years in the Palestine area. They thought the world was in need of them to solve its problems. We gave them the identification - false christs - as we compare their claims and works to those that describe the true Messiah. Another One of those men also appeared in Beit Jala where I lived. One day his mother and sister came to ask me to try to bring him back to himself as they put it. His mother cried as she said, "He's going crazy, please, could you do us a favor."

"Exactly, what does he do?"

"He has locked himself in a small room for two years now. Nobody is allowed to visit him or talk to him except those who approach him for healing. And he does that. He performs miracles".

"Did you or any body else observe any super natural, superhuman signs or movements?"

"Yes from time to time, after midnight, his room would shine and become brighter than sunshine on a clear summer day. Voices were heard then. I can't tell what it was. But it was fearful."

"That's enough. I will go to him one of these nights. Do not worry".

"Oh my dear neighbor", her daughter interrupted, "don't go please."

"What makes you ask me that?"

"I don't want you to get hurt."

"What 'do you mean?"

"He might hurt you, or put a spell on you. He did it to people we sent to him. He made them motionless as they tried to bring him back to his old self. Fortunately, and only after he released them, they could move and go home, having accomplished no results from their visit."

"Did he hurt any body physically?"

"Not exactly. But those strong young men we sent to him, as they got up and started on him to correct him by a good beating, he put a spell on them that they could not move."

"Then?"

"They pleaded, please loosen us and let us go. Smiling, he told them - OK go. And only then could they leave."

"Please," said his sister "don't go to him."

"No, no, I'll go, I promise. But I will go equipped. Don't you worry about me."

"What do you mean - equipped?"

"Having faith in God. And that Jesus is with me. I will not fight like other people."

I had chosen one of those nights to visit him in the realization that he too belonged to Jesus through that great sacrifice on Calvary. He too should be told the story of his Savior. I knocked at his outer gate at about 8pm. A voice was heard saying: "Come in Mr. Azar. Push the door. It is open. After you come in, turn to your right and open that other door where you will find me waiting for you."

To this day I do not believe he was fully aware of my visit to him at that time. If that happened to you, would you have entered into that house? Few have the courage to visit with such persons. Sometimes it is dangerous. Though, those who are ready at any moment to lay down their lives for their Savior will not be frightened whatsoever.

I followed his instructions to find myself at last face to face with the one claiming to be the Messiah. What to say, and how to start, had all belonged to God. He has promised to help in difficult times.

That visit lasted four and a half hours. And though the man was looked upon as a great man endowed with that supernatural power, yet he needed someone to confide in.

"How are you brother?" I asked.

"I'm alright brother Azar. This life consists of continuous war and struggle. What is that you are having in your hand?"

"It is the Bible."

"Why did you bring it with you, for war? Give it to me."

"No, I have my Bible and you have yours."

"Yes, people don't understand me. They don't appreciate me now."

"I understand you brother. We are alike, fighting in this life, trying to help those we meet from day to day. This is my Bible, God's book that I have with me. That is what is always in my hand."

He said, he planned to stop death and erase sin from the world but could not because his family interrupted him by waking him up from his vision. I said, "they are to blame, but what did you do so far?" He pointed to a corner in that room, where he wanted me to see Lucifer, where he tied him as a first step. I said that I believed him and did not need to see Lucifer. He said, "brother Najeeb, what miracle do you want me to perform so that you believe me?" I said that I did not need a miracle.

"Why not?" He said.

I told him that Jesus predicted that false Messiahs and profits would come and do miracles. He asked, "Do you consider me one of those false Messiahs?" I said, I hope that you are not.

"Alright," He said, "doesn't your book say that you can move mountains by faith?"

"Yes it does."

He said, "Perform a miracle for me."

I said, "Brother Mike, if you don't want to believe except by miracle, God is not going to do that for you and you are the loser. Neither do I need any miracles. The mountain mentioned resembles the sin in my heart and yours that we need to remove."

He said, "It seems that your book can do nothing." He pulled a book out of his pocket and said, "My book can do miracles." He placed an empty Kettle on the floor and said, "What do you want me to fill it with? You can ask for anything." I told him that I needed no miracles.

Brother Mike, I understand that you have a wife and five daughters and that your mother cleans houses for others in order to support your family." He agreed. I continued, "Brother Mike, you are the man who is supposed to work and support your family. Why don't you leave this very hard task for Jesus. He will do a better job. You said, you are getting tired, wont you give in to God."

In the course of that visit, he tried twice to put a spell on me or end my life by mumbling. I shook all over and right away turned to my Bible to open it and ask for help. He later said, had it not been for that book in your hand, I would have finished you.

"Brother Najeeb", he pleaded towards the end of the visit, "will you please pray for me?"

"O yes, of course."

"I feel as though I am going crazy. I don't know what or how to think. I want to come back to our God."

"OK, brother Mike I will pray for you now with the understanding that you will go out of this room and that you will do some shopping for your family tomorrow. Also, that you will start looking for a regular job. That you will work as an honest and good family member."

"Yes I will," he said.

"Now kneel brother and let us pray."

He could not rise just then. I extended my hand to lift him up. As he got up, I heard a crackling sound coming out from his knees. He knelt then and a prayer was offered to God to praise Him for the victory. He became a new and upright man there and then, a new creature in

Jesus Christ. His outward, worldly looks changed, and Christ the Lord began to live His life within him.

According to his promise he began his new life the very next morning, and lived a good and happy life thereafter.

Starting A School For Four Students

Next, I had a call to join the working force in Lebanon. The conference board advised that I should follow the interest aroused in Aramoun El-Gharb to the south of Beirut. Citizens of that village were composed of Christians and Druze, an Islamic sect, who lived in peace and loved one another. It was a challenge to preach the message and at the same time keep the unity of these dear people.

When I arrived I was introduced to the believers who were happy and excited to have a minister live with them for the first time. They had hoped and prayed *for* some body to encourage and pray with them. Meetings started and more and more people began to attend. They asked to be visited in their homes. They enjoyed singing, and visiting them formed a circle of meetings conducted every night of the week. Wherever I went, they asked to sing. Singing led to reading God's word. That was followed with some explanation of what was read. All would end with a prayer.

All of the Christian homes were visited, because all of them asked for visiting. Everybody was happy. When you sing, you feel happy. If singing makes you happier, why not sing all the time!

Some suggested that a school be started for the church members' children who counted only four. It was hard to get the conference to agree and approve the opening of a school for four pupils. And then to assume the responsibility of starting it meant providing room for that. The room should be offered by one of the church members. The conference had no budget for our project.

Our church leading cannon member offered one of his rooms to be used as a school. It had a bench for those four children to sit on. When you have only a few pupils, you can give them the best you have. And I believe that when you give those pupils entrusted into your care your very best, you will be rewarded with more pupils. The generous man's name was Farjalla.

The first month ended with twenty pupils. We had to rent a bigger room and furnish it with benches and a table for the teacher. The conference furnished those. At the end of the second month we had forty pupils.

The conference had to provide another teacher to help out. Most of the school children attended Sabbath School and church worship. Some parents started to show interest in the principals of the church. Later we had to move into a bigger building. Indeed we had a small beginning, and God blessed it.

Some parents who were prejudiced turned against their children because they attended our meetings continuously. One of those children was George. His father who advised him not to come to our meetings beat him more than once.

Often, persecution can make the persecuted more determined to follow their convictions. It is not wise to oppose those in your family who appear to be choosing to follow their own way in life. In most instances, those trying to force their own way on their beloved people will lose them. (Read Acts of the Apostles 5:37-40.)

George decided to be baptized into the faith he had adopted and now loved. Previous to that, his father told him that if he joined our church, he wouldn't include him in his benefits as a son and that he would not get his share of the inheritance. That did not stop George from following his Savior the way he chose. Before his baptism he came to me as his Pastor to ask for advice.

"George," I said, "it is up to you to decide. Be sure God loves you and wants the best for you and your salvation. The future is in His hands. It is difficult to disobey your father. Do your best to explain your faith to him and share with him your reasons for wanting to join this church." He did his best. It did not help any. So the day the boy joined the church, his father put him out of the house. The man was determined, and that was final.

The newly born son came back to tell me, "I am out of my father's house, no longer a son."

"George, do you accept to live with me in my home until God shows you another way out? I will be very happy to have you here." We lived together some days until I had a chance to go to The Middle East College located in Beirut, Lebanon. There I had a chat with the president about George's problem. He had no money that he could be admitted into college. Those who had the means and could sponsor him already had many other peoples to care for.

The president suggested that giving him a place to live and work could make a difference for him. He could work for his room and board. George was happy for the offer. Soon he was able to take one or two subjects the first semester.

He had to work his way through the entire process. It was very difficult managing his work, his living and his studies all the way until the day he graduated with his BA in Theology. After that he was given a church to Pastor. Later he resumed his studies until he got his PHD in Theology. As I left the Middle East with my family in 1973, George was teaching at the Middle East College.

His relationship with his father grew nicely And his father saw what kind of a man his son turned out to be by following his Lord and Master, he changed his mind. He built a house for George in Beirut, and they are now very good friends. His father became a wonderful friend of mine as well.

Here is another example of how people accept persecution happily as a result of following the way they believed God wanted them to be - is the following:

Nawal was a student in the Aramoun Al-Gharb School. As a result of studying God's word she faithfully followed her Savior. We missed her more than once in the church services, and I went to visit her. In the Middle East a church Pastor should always visit his church members. Some might for a reason or another be discouraged or offended. Some are sick. All need God's word read to them and everyone needs prayer.

Some families have problems between husbands and wives, or with their children. Those need counseling and everyone hopes for possible solutions. The Pastor's visits are looked for and expected. If a minister stops visitation, he should expect his people to stop coming to church.

Nawal would not give a reason for her absence from church. "Are you offended in any way Nawal," I said, "is there anything I could do to help you?"

"I love the Lord", she said, "but I cannot come to church". Later I learned that her mother was against her and persecuted her bitterly for her new faith. Next day I visited that good lady. Both she and myself were responsible for her daughter's education and character. We were both interested in her progress as a young woman and her personal welfare.

"I came to visit you Madam", I began, "and discuss your daughter's progress and character with you. How is Nawal doing."

"She is very good in her studies and school assignments, very kind and sweet in her character. She's only not good to me."

"What do you mean?"

"She doesn't obey me"

"You mean she does not help you with the everyday work around the house. She should be able to help some."

"No, that is not what I mean. She really does help me with the housework everyday with the exception of Saturdays, when I am left all alone as she goes to church."

I asked her, "What excuse does she give for leaving you all alone on that particular day?"

"That her God is displeased if she works on Saturday."

"Now, I know that Nawal is an exceptionally mature girl. She has taken that after her mother. It is hard though to be sincere and faithful to her God and her very generous Mother when they do not agree on these points of interest. Your help is so much necessary that Nawal could easily take over such responsibilities. If you promise to appreciate your wonderful daughter, and will help her keep up her obligations to God I'll tell you a secret. The more loyal our children are to God, the better they are in every walk of their life and we become the happier parents."

"You are right", said her mother. "I've been very cruel to Nawal. I have given her beatings. I have been shouting at her, and I have called her bad names. She doesn't deserve that kind of treatment from a mother."

"What do you plan to do now, will you change your attitude, and make it a more pleasant experience for your daughter to be happy with you?" Her answer was in the responsive way.

Nawal was free to worship and serve when that visit concluded. Both her Mother and her God loved her and she was left to love her God the way she wanted. She grew to be a real good lady. Later she joined M.E. College where acquaintance was made with a Christian young man of like faith and interests. They married and led a very happy life. Today that family enjoys life with their children in the USA.

Among the first four children who created the school in its beginning were Joseph and Elias both are now doctors. Joseph graduated majoring in education and teaching at M.E. College, and Elias majored in medicine and conducts his medical practice and his service to God in the USA.

When I Heard God's Voice

It was a winter day when I came down from Aramon El-Gharb to Beirut on business for the school. It was scheduled that I would get back after dark and hold worship that night. The only bus that ran between the capital and my residence usually leaves Beirut at 2 p.m. Taking advantage of the extra time before leaving, I left my suitcase on the bus, and went to buy a couple of batteries for my Torch light. I didn't know why I had that intention recognizing my old batteries were still good. Neither did I know why I held on so tightly to my umbrella.

Five minutes before the hour, coming to the bus stop, I found that it had already left. I discovered that a bus would be coming from another bus stop and another bus would leave later to the same district of the south, and it would stop not far from Aramoun. That was a different route going through different villages loading and unloading. One of those junctions where it stopped leads to Aramoun through mountains. And it shouldn't take more than 20 minutes walking. The bus stopped at that junction and I stepped down and began walking. Several passengers joined me as I walked.

It was raining during that time until it stopped when I arrived at the junction. I took that as an intervention by God's providence, that I could use my umbrella as a stick to lean on instead of protecting myself from the rain. It got dark soon after I had begun walking and I lost my way. In the dark, walking in valleys, you need a stick to lean on, and a Flashlight to guide your feet. When the rain stopped, the umbrella took the place of the stick. The Torch I had, had new batteries I was convinced these were signs of God's care and kindness for me. After

31

dark I was left alone without those other passengers who had come down from the bus with me. They had all headed in the direction of their respective destinations.

I began wandering among those mountains and into another valley. I had been walking for about one hour. I felt something was wrong. The distance I was hoping to travel should have taken only about twenty minutes.

"Why not go back," I reasoned within myself. And I turned and walked back towards the spot I had come from, hoping to find any sign of life, people, houses, fire, a dog barking, anything. I needed, I wanted help, somebody to direct me to tell me where I should go. That change of direction took another 30 minutes or so. Two big mountains stood now on both sides of me, with me walking in the valley between them. At the time went on, fear grew in me. Another idea ran through my mind, "I should go back to where I was, and continue down that direction until I come to the main road, the one connecting Beirut, the capital of Lebanon, with the other communities in the south."

I decided I would wait there on that road until a car would come from the south heading for Beirut, and then I will ask them to give me a lift. I thought I'd stay over night at the capital, and go to Aramoun the next day. The batteries I previously had bought were still very strong and a saving Grace. They showed me where to go and helped in driving away from me those wild beasts that lurk on the darkened roadways in Lebanon. Praised be the name of the Lord.

Two hours passed, and I was still lost. "Najeeb" I told myself, "you are lost, why don't you stop right here and now. The gracious God will send you guidance."

"Lord, I'm lost, would you please show me what to do, where to go? Please, kindly answer me. Thank you in Jesus' name." When I was just concluding that prayer I heard a voice coming from the mountaintop which was to my right. That voice I could never, and will never be able to describe. It was full of love, great concern, and warning.   It said:

"Najeeb! Najeeb!"

"Yes," I answered, "Who are you, who is calling?" that was all I heard. The voice must be warning me from some dangers ahead. I turned backward until another half an hour passed. What am I going to do? Should I go back? Wait, pray again"

And again I prayed. The same voice called again from the same direction with the same warning tone in its voice "NAJEEB! NAJEEB!" - Back I went downward to the river determining to continue until I reached the main road that led to Beirut. This time it took a bit more than half an hour. Suddenly I came to a place where I could not go farther. It was so dark, my torchlight failed to show me where to put my next foot. The light itself was still very strong. I could not understand how it showed clearly, in all directions except this one directly in front of me. It was so very strange and frightening; in such a way I had never felt so very afraid in my life. I needed to pray again for I knew not what to do, or where to go. I offered the same prayer, and the same voice was heard warning me the third time.

"Lord," I decided, "I'll follow the direction your voice came from, help me, I need you now as never before." I began climbing that mountain. I don't remember how long it took me. The mighty Lord endowed me with extra strength. When I reached the top of that mountain, I heard somebody calling:

"Who is it?" The voice asked.

"A friend," I answered. That ought to be the answer you should give if you were in similar circumstances in the Middle East. You wouldn't want to be suspected of being an enemy or a thief. Otherwise the person calling might most assuredly shoot you and you might be killed, it would be your fault.

"What do you want here this time of the night, and, where are you going?" said the suspicious man.

I told him who I was, that I was lost and wanted to go to Aramoun. "Sir, I asked, did you call me by my name moments ago?"

"No, but come in with me to my house and have something hot to drink. Warm yourself up a bit, he said and later I'll show you the way to Aramoun."

"Thank you very kindly. But if you want to be helpful to me, just show me where to go. My people are waiting for me and it has gotten very late." I was later told that my church members, my students, and some friends wondered why only my suitcase had arrived that afternoon.

They took it for granted that I was lost, and prayed that I could find my way back to them. I did reach them that night, with the help of the suspicious gentleman. As I told them about what had happened to me, and as I mentioned that spot where my light failed to show me where to go, they looked to one another and with tears in their eyes they proposed that we all kneel and give thanks to the gracious Lord, the God I prayed to then, and followed the voice instead of continuing downwards.

"Why?" I asked.

"Because," one of them said, "had you continued to walk on in the direction you were going, you would have had walked directly into a much feared area of quicksand in the area. And surely you would have died."

We praised the God of heaven and earth and gave thanks to Him for His care and protection.

Away from and with God
1947 - Another new beginning

Having started the school at Aramoun, and by His grace won some precious souls to the Savior, comments began to come both by letters and in person. In the past I had not been well recommended, but now that I was closer to the presidency, the results of my work received more direct attention and were appreciated.

One of those letters that commended on my work came from G.A. Keough who included the following words in his kind commentary. "As though you were hidden under a bushel."

Everything looked bright and promising until the day when I was told to go to the head office at Beirut. I expected good news. I was doing really well. I was gaining recognition for my work. I was already spreading my activities and endeavors to other villages and towns in the district with good and encouraging results. People everywhere were eager to hear the gospel message. It was enjoyable to walk those long roads from one town to the other in beautiful Lebanon.

As I entered into that office, three officers were there to pass on to me the news. The man who had sent me that letter was one of the men waiting for me in the office. The committee had chosen those three men to tell me what had been voted concerning me in that session of the committee's deliberations. One of them said "Brother Najeeb we know you've been working very hard and faithfully, and have had good results so far. But we've been asked by the executive committee to ask you to find work outside the Mission. I was being fired, let go and defrocked. I was crushed. Every word felt like a

35

sharp and heavy stone thrown by my peers, and landing on my body, as if in punishment by stoning for committed sin. I trembled, and said:

"If sin has been the reason for the action this committee is taking, I want to know right now, what is it that I am accused of, and who is the accuser. I want to ask God and the person I had sinned against for forgiveness. Not for the sake of work, but I want to make things right with my God."

"No it is no sin."

The real reason behind it was, that the president of the Union, being influenced by a certain, influential lady, wanted me to get married. I was 27 years old, and it was thought that it was time that I should marry. They had taken it upon themselves to decide this very important matter for me, without me.

However, what they did not know was that there was nothing on earth that could force me to marry that girl. There had been no affair and no dating with that girl. And because I did not love her in any sense that would indicate that I would refuse their thoughtful proposal. The president in turn influenced the committee members that I should either accept their wise and good advice or be asked to find work outside the organization. They hoped that such a strategy would convince me of the wisdom of their efforts on my behalf.

Although I was in that age, I felt I was obligated to my widowed mother after the death of my father, as well as to my brothers and sisters in Jordan, and would help them financially. That was my guiltless guilt.

"Before leaving the mission work, I addressed the committee representatives. I said "I would like to express my thanks and appreciation to the Mission and their representation of it for the kindness and love I have always got from them all. I ask you to please pray for me as I now move into this new chapter of Gods Plan for my life."

They said they were happy that I took it so nicely, and reported the same to the committee. That action precipitated them to propose that I receive six months salary, one month for each of the six years I had served. I chose to receive that amount on a monthly basis. Those six months I spent in preaching and giving Bible studies. I thought I should not receive unearned money. They considered it, according to their terminology, indemnity for the former six years of my service. I also hoped they would change their mind and somehow reverse their action of dismissal since I had only been guilty of saying no to their poorly considered proposition.

The committee members would not reconsider my case, making it one of those Medo-Persian Laws from (Daniel 6:8). The indemnity period extended from April till September 1948. Israel was taking over in Palestine and all of history was about to change.

During that time I made several visits to the Brazilian Consulate in Beirut. I asked them if I might immigrate to Brazil. I explained my finances, my case with the Mission, and my background. The Brazilian Consul demonstrated much kindness and concern in my case and promised to help me.

"If you apply for citizenship, I'll help you get it and consider you a visitor here in Lebanon, and in one month's time send you back to your country. You have to pay some money for that."

"Thank you very kindly Sir. I would be grateful if you would do this for me." He told me the procedure would cost twenty-five Lebanese pounds, which I was ready to pay. But again, feeling with me, he said, never mind, I'll pay that for you.

During that same period I used to visit a relative of mine living at Aitha El-Fukhar, Bekaa, Lebanon. The people of that village became interested in the way I lived as a Christian, and wanted the same kind of life for their children. They learned I was both a teacher and preacher so they asked me to start a school there. "I can't do that." I said. "I am not a part of the Mission anymore, and therefore I am without the necessary equipment for such a wonderful undertaking."

"Never mind," they protested, "you can still start a school for us, and we're ready to help you out."

"You mean though I have no desks, no chairs, no black- boards and no books, you still insist on having me do it?"

"That's right, work out a plan and bring it to us, and let us discuss it and consider how to do it. Will you?"

I made my plan and it consisted of three simple but vital considerations:

1. Every pupil would provide his or her own chair to sit on.

2. Every pupil would buy the necessary books and stationary he or she needed.

3. Monthly education fees would be paid in full at the start of every month.

I confess. I purposefully made those fees just a little bit higher than needed so that I might earn the necessary money to immigrate to Brazil. And I knew that I would have it paid for in just one month. All of my conditions were unanimously accepted. Then I traveled to Al-Husn, Jordan to say goodbye to my mother, my brothers and sisters. This would be our last time together. It was too hard for them to accept the reality that I was leaving them for good.

Letters from Aitha followed me to Jordan, asking me to go to them and start that school right away. It should be started in September, and in a few days I went back to Lebanon. My plans were that I would stay with my sister Nabeeha, her husband and children in Beirut. There I would get ready and immigrate to Brazil.

Early in September I headed towards the consulate to complete the final procedures. On my way I accidentally met one of the Aitha people who had sent the letters to me.

"Man," he said, "they are all asking for you, where have you been? Come on with me, they're waiting for you"

"OK brother, I said, I'll come in a little while."

"Where are you going?"

"Somewhere to see a friend of mine, have lunch, and then come back to you?"

"No, as for your friend, you'll see him some other day. And you and I will have lunch together, and together we will go to Aitha. I am supposed to ask you to accompany me if I happen to meet you. Our people will be happy if you come now."

He would not let me go and I could not resist. It looked like a spell had been put on me. At that moment I paused to think, and I said to myself: "I asked that God's hand would lead and guide me!" Well there I was heading for the consulate, and then there I was heading towards Aitha, with a very determined servant of God in the lead.

We arrived at Aitha that afternoon. The next day, I registered 47 pupils comprising grades 1 through 6.

My trip to the consulate never materialized and school had begun.

I rented a furnished apartment that very day for myself, and two rooms for school use. If you should ask me about my financial background or my budget at that time, I'd tell you it was either a zero or faith. Who would start a project like this in such a foolish way? Would you act on in Faith?

Nowadays we see domestic and international missions and denominations wavering, having not enough courage to spread the gospel news just a little further. They claim they do not have the budget and strength to accomplish such a good work for God. Isn't that a shame? Aren't we all lucky the apostles were fools for their faith, and welded to the ideal of the Cross? That next day I was on my way back to Beirut to buy books and stationary for my school. When I arrived I went to Musaitbih School, the main Seventh Day Adventist School, to ask it's principal for a loan of 250 Lebanese pounds.

"Could I ask you what you want the money for?"

"Yes," I said, "I am starting a school and I am here to buy books and stationary. I promise to bring back your money in 2 days."

"A school, where and how could you do it?"

"You'll know later. Just give me the money if you have it."

"OK, let me see what we have in the safe here."

"No please, don't do that. I want the money to come from your own pocket, not from the school." He said

"I understand you well. Never mind but suppose I go down with you to the bookshop and give my name as a reference. You'll get a special reduced price, which will be for your convenience. He was a friend of mine. I accepted his offer, carried my goods and went back to Aitha that same day.

Every pupil was expected to buy the needed books and stationary before school started. Another teacher should be hired right away to help out. I did that hiring the first day. The government school principal with his three staff teachers visited me that evening to mock me.

"You really hope to sell all of this that you bought?" said the principal, "I haven't been able to solicit enough money to buy a broom for our school. They never buy books."

In one day everyone at our new little school of 47 students bought and paid for their books and each of their sets of stationary. And yes they brought their chairs, each of them and all of the fees were collected just as promised.

Realize with me, in this wonderful recollection, how God rewards His children when they have faith in His promises. The day the school started was both funny and enjoyable. Every one of the children picked up his or her chair and placed them beside one another against the schoolroom walls, leaving the middle part of the room vacant. This was done so that the pupils might lean up against the wall because none of the chairs had a back. They were what the British and the Americans called stools. We called them straw chairs. Whenever they needed to write, they would use their bookcases as desks.

The full time teacher I hired was the son of the Orthodox priest. He was the only priest for the only church in Aitha, even though they had several church buildings which were used on different occasions for different events there was only one priest for this entire community. Along with that teacher called Adeeb, I hired a part time woman teacher to teach the girls Home Economics. When I went to ask her to teach for me, she asked how much she would be paid? I asked her whether she wanted to learn the English language? She said yes. So I said what about trading teaching for me in return for learning the English Language? She agreed.

For Physical Education, I would use my accordion, which made it so interesting and enthusiastic. Many would come out from their homes to watch their children march and play. The school was going on so successfully that the government school principal was aroused with prejudice. He started persecuting this new set up. Though the more confusion he stirred, the fewer pupils he had left in his own school. Later the education ministry thought to take away members of his staff of teachers and use them elsewhere.

Our school grew, and residents of Aitha started asking for some religious programs that would be worked out by their children. As Christians they loved to see their offspring grow up both academically and spiritually.

The only place I could have such programs acted would be one of those two churches in the town, pastured by the one priest. I was told I must visit the Bishop about such matters, but that he was not around a great deal. However I was told that if I could not speak with him about it I should know that the priest was on the church board and that his son was a teacher in our school. I spoke to the priest and he agreed kindly to let me have the larger church building for our programs. We were allowed to keep the church's keys for eight days, which was very unusual. It was well decorated and the children practiced their parts most satisfactorily. It was a Christmas program with songs, holy carols and recitals.

The day the program was performed, the church was too small to hold all of those that wanted to attend. Even until now, after all of these years, the people there in Aitha still remember that day and wish to have the children's programs resumed. Maybe they felt that way because all their girls who were very beautifully dressed for the occasion got married.

Every home in Aitha was visited and rounds were made every night over one section and then another to see that the children did their homework. Those who had some difficulties in their studies were helped. As a result, all those who were scheduled at the end of the school year for government examinations passed successfully and got their certificates.

That school continued there approximately two years. One of the good results was that most of the best students in Lebanon at that time, according to government statistics, belonged to our fine little school in Aitha.

News of our school spread near and far. The mission head office, from which I had been dismissed heard about our successes. The representative officials of the Mission committee began traveling to Aitha, to spy as it were. It was such a phenomenon, it looked as if it were a miracle. They went into that two room school, with no chairs, desks, blackboards, tables, and a bell. You see everyone took their school supplies home, as I did mine, each and every night. When the Committee Representatives arrived they spied through empty rooms that were evidently producing "miracle" students.

The church board granted the two rooms we used for the second year. Prior to us using them, they had been used exclusively for the girls' school. When we arrived we did not create a separation between the boys and the girl's rooms and we took advantage of that increased exposure in our learning.

As the Mission's officials came in to visit our strange little school, they wondered how in the world such a thing could ever happen. Again they read the weekly schedule, which had five separate curriculums starting with Monday.

"Brother Azar what do you do on Saturdays and Sundays?" To them, pure religion consisted of keeping that day (Saturday) separate and apart from all other considerations.

"Saturdays we have a short worship in the morning, and Sundays are free days." I said.

"How many Adventist members do you have, in this town?" "One" I replied, and made sure they understood it to be me. "How could you start this school?" they asked. And as I am sure you know, if someone is inclined to ask such a question, the answer you have to give will never satisfy their inquiry. I will give you a little example of something I was to learn of many years later.

A young pastor and his wife were given a post in a tiny church (just 7 people), in a place faraway from the beaten paths of society. They had two children and were, by earthly standards quite poor. They did not come equipped with great denominational provisions but came equipped with extra-earthly provisions of abiding faith and trust in God and a well, studied knowledge of God's Word. Three years later, while receiving an international award before a few thousands of their fellow pastors, for being one of the top three Missionaries raising churches in America for this well known denomination they were asked how it was that their church had become almost 10% of the population of their community, and had been able to give all of that money year by year to missions.

The young pastor answered with these very words. "We were told that Christ builds His church. We knew that if that was true then all we would have to do was show up, teach His Word, and serve His Body and that He would take care of the rest. And obviously He did."

Letters began to come, some asking me whether I wanted Supplies sent to help me with our worship in the school.

I answered that it seemed to be the same with or without supplies, that I did have my Bible and that the people did not seem to care that we did not have hymnals or an organ or organist. I should confess I did say that out of bitterness.

Now that we were a success everyone wanted to be a part of that glory. Even in my bitterness, the supplies started coming anyway. A letter dated December 27, 1950 signed by the committee representative said:

"I am very glad to be able to report to you what the Union Committee thinks about the good work you are doing over there, and to show you how much they appreciate the work you have been doing, they are going to give you some assistance."

That help consisted mostly of helping me with the medical debt that was standing against me as a result of the sickness I had while working at Addar near Karak in Jordan. They also paid the sum of 250 Lebanese pounds that had been given to me, as help for the school.

Another letter came from the same man agreeing to let me have some other school equipment to help in our classrooms. Later another president proposed that the school would be in a better shape now with those supplies brought in assuring another new beautiful start, especially if it was followed up by the denomination. In east Lebanon we had no other shcool.

We Christians, so often fail to seize the opportunities provided by God, as they come in different parts of the world. When missions started around the world, they started by faith. They were poor in their beginnings, both the organizations and their servants. As they followed holding God's own hand, and his powerful will implemented in their mission fields (His Mission Fields) God prospered His work. It was His work then and it is His Work now. As they followed on after God, they got rich. And following the riches, not too much later, their only concern then and now has been ways and means to keep and increase their riches. Faith is dying out, taking a backseat to earthly economics and practicality. His work as it becomes ours will die as well. Satan has now begun to rule in many churches, removing faithful confidence. Removing our trust in God's mercy and those promises emanating from His own Heart to the hearts and minds of His children, replacing that with a crippling dependency on denominational heresies and the love of Money.

Becoming my own physician

Mount Hermon (now called Jabal el-Shaik) is not far from Aitha. It always has white peaks, with snow staying there all year. Living at Aitha, I used to climb up to some of those heights every morning. There I started my day in meditation and prayer. It is very cold up there. And as a result of those exercises in the very early mornings, I developed a backache. On the run it used to knock me over. For eight years physicians could not discover what it was that was claiming my strength. Whenever their prescriptions suggested guesses and trials I would buy those medicines. Some suggested tablets or liquids for my stomach thinking it was the cause of my backache.

I did not want to have more than one physical problem. I remembered that lady Jesus healed from bleeding which accompanied her twelve years. The Holy record states that she suffered from many physicians rather than from her sickness.

It is difficult and can even be fatal to give yourself over to a doctor who would only guess your problem and then give the treatment. Eight years later, in 1958 as I was going back home to Ramallah, Palestine, I thought of treating myself my own way. This would not be taking some medicine internally. A simple backache plaster might solve the problem. So I just called at a drug store and bought one of those plasters, and brought it home.

"Will you please help me honey," I asked my wife, "apply this plaster on my back just where I have the pain."

"Has a physician prescribed it for you?"

"I did the prescribing, why not, everyone else has had their unsuccessful guesses why not me?" Half an hour after applying that plaster, my pain left me forever. I continued using those plasters one after the other for three months. And thanks to the gracious Lord for His wonderful love and care, I had no more pain.

Letters kept coming to me asking me to rejoin the Mission. They would not accept that I stay where I was. Rather they had a problem for me to solve. My work was assigned that I go back to my hometown and build up the work of the church, which was going downward. Church members were no longer churchgoers.

That was both a challenge and an obligation. I accepted the call, and I had to give up that wonderful work in Aitha.

24-Hour Witness in a Syrian Prison

On my way from Lebanon to Jordan, the following event happened as I entered into the Syrian Custom's house between Lebanon and Syria. As any other passenger, my luggage was inspected. They wanted to make sure that passengers carried no weapons, or any forbidden substance. Among my belongings they found a copy of the Sabbath School Senior quarterly booklet. They were issued four times a year, including weekly lessons, and were used whenever there was a church that belonged to the same organization. Those lessons were studies conducted and taught every Saturday, therefore they were known as Sabbath School quarterlies, while the other Christian churches call such publications Sunday School Lessons. Saturday, in Arabic is pronounced and written as "Sabbath." The same day and the same word belonged to the Jews who lived in Palestine, very close to the other Arab countries.

Sunday was generally accepted as the day Christians should have as their day of worship. On reading that heading on that booklet, the officer right away asked whether I was a Seventh Day Adventist.

"Yes I am." I said. I was kept in the office with my belongings, while the car driver was ordered to leave.

After some phone calls were made between the Custom's house and the police head office in Damascus, I was sent accompanied by two soldiers to that huge Syrian city. There I was taken to jail. I had not committed a crime. I had not done anything, except that I belonged to that church. I would have to stay in jail as long as it took them to investigate and decide what to do in my case.

Every now and then I was called out in order to answer their many questions and give a reason of the kind of faith I had. How happy I was that, I had no time to lie down and sleep during my 24 hours in jail. It wasn't convenient any way, because I would have had to sleep with only a blanket, on a narrow bench. And it was my blanket. Also, many officials were required, owing to their positions, to ask me about my faith. This made it possible for me to witness to many of them who were on a very high level politically in the dear country of Syria. Many of these men became my friends. They enjoyed hearing me explain my faith as a Christian. Some chose to cancel their appointments for that night preferring to stay with me. I talked so much and often about the way a true Christian lived and how and why we considered ourselves God's elect in this world. It appeared as a new and strange faith to them. They could find out we were sound in what we believed, because we were in our doctrines, the closest Christian sect to Islam. We were in agreement on many points of belief.

If those people who were in charge of the mission work in Syria at that time could only show better understanding, exercise common sense and use the right approach, many good and kind Muslim peoples might find their way into the arms of Christ.

I still remember the last interview I had with the second most important man in that department as I was called upon to answer those many questions, which were asked over and over by each of the interrogators, he said:

"Now tell me about you, all of your life." the officer said.

"Where shall I start, I answered, the moment I was born or when?"

He gave it a smile and said, "Since you started going to school."

That was a long story and my file grew bigger every second. "I will limit myself to the most important things for you to record in your book," I said. One of my questions to him was "Why did you arrest me? I am a Jordanian. If by any means you suspect me of any violence, as to whether I am a Jew or a Zionist, you could notify my country. Why should I be questioned like this?" Instead of getting angry he was extremely kind and answered it wouldn't be long before I would be released.

I spoke again, "I consider myself your guest. I have been without food for 24 hours now. Would you please order one of your men to buy me something to eat? I will pay for it."

He would not. He said that it wouldn't be long before I was released. He was right, though they kept most of my books. The promise was that after they went through them, they would send them to my address, which they wrote and attached to the big bag they put them in. In fact those books were selected on their request from the other books that were allowed to accompany me. The officer could not tell which book would tell something worthy about Seventh Day Adventists. His English was limited. Still those that remained were important to me. I had read them and reread them, marked, and underlined them the way I liked it. So I did not want to lose my treasures.

Shortly afterwards I was led by a soldier who took me to all those who shared in writing my life story into their journals, one by one. Every one of them would take off his part of the report from my file, until my passport was left clean and without contrary remarks. The last man, however, wanted to write on it that I should leave the country in 24 hours.

"No please", I interrupted," instead, of giving me that long time to go on my way why not write that I should leave without delay?" He handed me my passport without writing anything on it. I had lunch at 2 p.m. and found a seat on a passenger car, and headed towards my country triumphantly and in peace.

Next morning I applied for my books through Jordan's Foreign Affairs Ministry. As I told my story to the governor, he felt bad that I was so badly treated and hurt by our sister country, and encouraged me to pursue my claim until I got those books back. It took one year until I could retrieve them. I was called upon to go all the way back to Damascus and get those books, which I reluctantly did.

In my hometown of Al-Husn, visitations started and meetings followed which resulted in giving Bible studies. That in turn ended with baptisms. Baptisms equipped the church with membership. Those members began asking that they have a school started for their children who would get the right education if they were in the right school. Members wanted their children to be taught the principles and religion they loved. In those countries, every school taught the kind of religion the owner of that school followed. In order to insure the education you want for your children, you would send them to your own church school.

Responding to the parents' request, a school was started. We could not limit ourselves to our own children because:

1. Outsiders should not be denied the privilege of getting the right education, in AI-Husn, the way we understand it.
2. Limiting ourselves would make us suspicious of taking such a stand against others.
3. We need to and should be friends to everybody.
4. Others would be offended if they should be left out and rejected.
5. The school would not fulfill its obligation as an evangelistic institution.
6. The work would grow and be better financed.

Everyone who applied to join the school, as a student, was accepted. Those who were too poor to pay the school fees were admitted free of charge. The school was looked upon as a true Christian school.

The teachers worked hard and were both zealous and faithful towards their sacred obligations. School children grew to love one another as brothers and sisters. Different activities, sports, and social gatherings made the school popular and increased its enrollment.

One morning a woman came to visit me, being in charge of the school as well as the church pastor. She came for counsel and help. A prayer was asked for her son who was discharged from all the schools he joined. She had no intention to ask that he be enrolled in our school, expecting the same outcome. He could never take anyone as a friend and was at the same time very hard to get along with. He loved no body, and nobody was interested in him. He would beat his own mother and sisters and call them bad names.

Often he would throw stones at them when things did not work in his favor and in his own way.

"OK", I said, "I'll pray for him, but again I would advise you to enroll him in our school. What about that?"

"Would you Pastor accept him for sure?"

"Yes, didn't I propose it?"

"But, this is wonderful. My son has nowhere else to go. He needs it so. I know your school is the solution, but I thought it was too good for my son."

"No sister, (Everybody is always considered either a brother or a sister by us, not only church members. Because, really, wasn't that God's plan from the beginning?), send your son to school right away."

"And", she said hesitantly, "You wouldn't discharge him?"

"I'll try not to."

Her son was sent to school. Special care was taken for him. And he, through Jesus' grace and Christian love turned out to be one of the best boys. Later, he was converted and joined the Middle East College where he studied for several years. As this is written, he is enjoying a wonderful family life and is well to do.

The youth were given special consideration. Both religious and social meetings were held for them. They read parts of famous speeches, recitations, and songs. And they were given opportunities to participate in programs. Their parents loved to come and watch their children perform their parts. If the young of the church are left out, they will grow careless and their talents even their faith can wither and die out. As a result the church will suffer and lose her youthful treasures. A church without its youth is soon to be a dead church.

We were more appreciated because of those many programs. The enrollment increased every month, and we had to rent a larger building. Later a church and school building was built in Al-Husn.

The young people were organized into groups for visitation from house to house. They also enrolled people in the VOP (Voice of Prophecy) Bible lessons. Every Saturday they were sent out to hold other Saturday School branches.

We soon had four of those in villages throughout the area. One of the visiting groups called on a family for the purpose of enrolling them in a Bible corresponding course. As a result the whole family accepted the gospel message and followed their Lord and Savior in baptism. It wasn't enough though to receive the lessons sent to them. Some of those lessons needed more explanation. There is also the importance of applying God's Word and living it. That family showed deep interest in what they studied. That in turn encouraged me to continue visiting them. Their son who recently immigrated with his wife and two children from Iraq to Washington State was the first opening to that family. He loved to join M.E. College and arranged for me to sit with his parents and elder brother and discuss his education problems. After they learned all the facts about M.E. College as I explained them to them, they agreed to send Foad to study there. Foad, being so interested in the Bible College began to write and invite his sister to join him the next year. She did for one year and a fraction of the second.

Finding The Girl Of My Dreams

Among the many families I got acquainted with at Aitha in Lebanon, there was one that had a daughter who had a growing interest in me. Although I really did not go on a date with her, yet she was in love with me and thought she'd be the right and only wife for me. I knew that through her letters to me after I left Lebanon. It didn't work out though because she was more interested in me than in my religion, which meant that much more to me. My new acquaintance with the Elaimy's Family (Foad's Family) on the other hand gave me another inspiration. Those people lived the life I admired and longed to cherish when I had a family. Every one of them loved the Lord and had his or her religion practically sound. The only obstacle in my way was that they be convinced I was not a Jew because of Saturday keeping. This has always been the offence to many good, sincere Christians. Jews were looked upon as the Arabs' number one enemy and nobody was supposed to have anything in common with them.

It took me a long time to prove to my new family the soundness of our belief as a church. As an organization I could never prove it to them.

The denomination sticks more to their policies than to the sincere doctrines of the faith itself. The good Lord led me one step at a time. Sometimes it looked as though all doors were locked in my face. Things did not work out that I could go to Brazil. Working in Aitha helped me financially though I had obligations towards my family in Jordan, which made it impossible for me to plan and work towards building my own family and future.

More than three times I had chance to marry a wealthy lady and I would not. I could never stand the fact of being dependant on my wife for living. In this I erred, because I learned later that a man could accept to be helped by his wife and enjoy the happiest of life. I never regretted though the chance I lost, since my final and only choice was the best.

The girl I had in mind to marry should never have been married before whether legally or illegally. Our culture and habits are closely related to the Holy Bible. That old, fashioned culture compels a single man if he is ever found involved with sex with an unmarried girl, to keep her as his legal wife. She had to accept him as her lawful husband. Otherwise she would be looked down upon (Read Lev. 18:20 & Duet. 22.) That again required love, because it was assumed that they would not have come together if they hadn't had feelings for one another. If a man raped a girl, he would be killed. If a man was caught with another man's wife in the very act of sex, and the woman did not cry out for help, both of them would be stoned to death. If that was done in a forest or away from people where no body could hear her when she cried, the man alone would be killed. However antiquated you might think these cultural laws are, they exist today and are a major part of the upbringing the social guidelines of those communities.

For instance, it is believed and followed that an Orthodox priest should marry a virgin. According to the Old Testament He is Holy unto the Lord and pure, his wife should be pure as well. In these present days pastors are performing the duties of the priests to a great extent. They preach the gospel and teach religion.

I thought since I occupied-such a position that I should have a virgin for wife. This would ensure the following benefits:

1. It would always, ever remind me of my holy calling and sacred responsibilities.
2. There, would be no memories of ex husband or ex- wife. I should be a virgin too. This was God's original plan. He gave one Eve to one Adam to stay together, forever.
3. Children would enjoy living with their real parents.
4. A united family's children would stay happy, with no fear of separation or divorce. They wouldn't be denied the privileges of the real family life.

Foad's family grew to be very dear and close to my heart. The way they lived, raised their children, and worshipped God. Many times it was hard to convince them about some doctrinal points. Whenever they got mixed up concerning the meaning of some biblical texts, they would turn to God in fasting and prayer. The most difficult two points they needed special guidance with were:

1. Keeping Saturday for Sabbath.
2. Whether they, as adults should be baptized the second time.

Through visions in the nights the mother was shown that she with her family decided to obey the Lord. The Ten old commandments appeared for her in the skies brilliant and shiny. From that she understood that they were still binding on those who wanted to follow God.

The second most difficult stand to take was again showed in another vision with both mother and children going into the Jordan River and coming out with white robes. The father of that family was never baptized.

He held some valid issues against the denomination itself. He thought there should be more love and sacrifice in their lives and actions. That it wasn't enough to see their followers, as he put it, exercise love and pay their tithes and offerings to the organization.

That family excluding the father began keeping Saturday for their Sabbath, attending every church service. And still considered it a great sacrifice for the Middle East church members to keep Saturday. And as I have mentioned before it is dangerous as well to be related to the Jews in any way. Through my study of the bible I discovered that the Sabbath was given to the Jews for a special purpose (read Dut. 5:15.)

Everyone, as soon as he or she joined that church had to be well equipped with biblical texts and proofs in order to answer those many objections.

The baptism of the Elaimy family was arranged to take place in the traditional spot where Jesus Christ our Lord was baptized. That day would never be forgotten. Three from that family took their stand and were buried with their Savior to rise with Him into a new life. A bus was rented for the occasion and both members and friends were in the baptism company. In the Middle East, people consider it an honor to be invited to join relatives and neighbors on special occasions.

That, at the same time, meant a great celebration to God's family, uniting more people to Him through such a spiritual marriage. Existing church members would at such an hour remember the time they took a similar step, and would renew their covenant with their Lord.

And those who never have had the opportunity to be baptized, would feel the need for it and respond to the call always made. Tears of joy could be seen running down on many faces.

More believers go through the spiritual ritual of dying and being born again. Every time baptism took place, many would be aroused to the desire of following their Savior. Those occasions worked marvelously towards increasing the membership in that part of the world, when we invited people and paid for them to come to the baptism. We really never lost financially. The wonderful Lord always rewards the Faith of His children. Praise His name.

After baptism was over, we usually had a pot-luck lunch and spent the rest of the day singing and having a good time together.

With that accomplished, the church was organized having enough members. The school went on successfully. We needed another teacher, and Najla, Foad's sister, was called upon to teach. She was one of those who were baptized that day. When she was asked to teach, she refused, and referred me to others whom she thought could do the job.

It was hard to convince her to accept the offer. Even though it was a wonderful job of service. Consecrated people are more sure and faithful in their work. That was a grand beginning and needed to be followed up with visitation and personal contacts. A minister who sits at his table, only to study, pray, and prepare his sermons, is never a successful worker for God in the Middle East. It should work out the same all over the world especially in America.

As the work was started and organized to go on in faith and hard labor, I was called to leave for another district to start new interests. That was never strange to me. I even anticipated such incidents. During my 32 years of ministry in that part of the world I was moved 27 times.

I always hated to leave the good starts the Lord helped me to make. Yet I never refused to move, and always found dear souls to work for and help find their Savior. Other members and friends in the north district of Jordan were not happy that I should leave.

God's thoughts are not like ours. He had his own reasons for each and every call.

Before moving to my new location, which was Karak this time, I thought that the time had come for me to start my family life. After Najla taught one year at the Al-Husn school, she joined her brother Foad at the Middle East College in Lebanon. My new post of duty in Karak would start around the beginning of 1955. The girl I dearly loved and wanted to have for a wife was then in Lebanon studying. Those quick transfers from one place to another made it necessary for me to think of having my own family. On the other hand I could not refuse those calls having the conviction that what the committee voted, was from God. He would be my best helper.

Also being one of those committee members made it clear that I was the man for the job. After that need was made clear to me, I could never reject. Traditional customs of the country involve the whole family when a daughter is asked for marriage. Father and Mother, brother and sister should all agree. All want to ensure happiness for everybody who is to get married whether a son or a daughter.

But our marriage is to be once and for life. Therefore everyone is concerned. It is not supposed to be a trial and liable to change. There is no divorce or separation in our cultural married, family life.

My first move according to our customs was, to send my mother to Najla's parents to ask them for their daughter's hand in marriage. It was as hard to convince them as it was for them to decide. It was also for their daughter to accept prior to her parents' positive agreement. Every thing should work out in harmony. After they have pronounced their blessing, almost all problems could be solved. My mother was not a persuasive kind of person. She accepted their reasons for not giving their daughter at that time. They thought she should study and graduate before marriage.

As for me, it was hard to be convinced when it came to my own choice in this matter in my life. So I had to rely both, on myself and on God, that all would be well. I struggled much, and succeeded in getting the approval of her parents. Soon after that, both her parents and I wrote to her to tell her of the news that she is engaged to me if it met her approval. I kept arguing with them for several nights until they got tired of arguing and gave their blessing and approval. She also agreed. I think she thought I was good for her as a husband. She agreed, however, after her older sister, who was not married yet, and her brother, who was working for an oil company in the Arabian Gulf, encouraged her. Culturally She was supposed to wait until that older sister is married before her. This is the custom over there, which again is taken from the Holy Bible. Respect is required from youngsters towards those who were older. But since that sister allowed and encouraged Najla to marry before her, she gave her final word and approval.

The wedding would take place on the 27th of December 1954, and it would be the first wedding performed in the Amman church ever. Three ministers officiated in our wedding. We went to Palestine for our honeymoon. We made Jericho our center and went to the different parts of the West Bank to visit. We went around and visited Jerusalem, Hebron, and Samaria (Nablus). We had a great time together.

I remember visiting Bethlehem where the church of the Nativity is located. We also visited Bethany where the, tomb of Lazarus stands witnessing to the power of Jesus raising the dead man to life. Again the pool of Bethesda where the 38-year sick man was brought back to health and strength. Concluding our short honeymoon, we had to go to the new post of duty assigned for us. That was Karak where I formerly started the work.

Nothing would work better than visitation. We focused at rebuilding the work under the guidance of the Holy Spirit, and start a day school. Wherever we went, people would ask for a school for their children. They wanted their youngsters to be taught the same principles their church held.

It was a wonderful idea to start a school. It would be the best way to help the church grow. A church without children is barren. It would be the best means *for* evangelism, to reach out for other very precious souls and help them get acquainted with their Lord and Savior, to love and serve Him. It is a happy church whose children are trained from their youth to serve their Master.

In order to start a school we needed to obtain two permits. One from the Mission head office which was the harder since it required committee action and budgets good enough to run the school and keep it going. The other permit we got easily from the local government.

We had to start with two rented schoolrooms, and two teachers and the church Pastor as the principle, I was happy to assume that responsibility along with my Pastoral obligations. The school grew and proved to be the best of all the schools in the city.

Many of the local government officials' children were enrolled in the school where they could acquire the right education they had been looking for. The daughters of the mayor were also included.

It is true that persecution occurred whenever something so right and good succeeds. And those difficulties always affect the ones who are the closest to the work. The hardest and most bitter ones are those, within our own community of Christ who were not able to reach the same levels through very much the same efforts. For this reason the church should be ready to act with compassion and treat her own members for their difficulties as if they were injured or ill people. If the church neglects such duties it will eventually crush its opportunities for the continued participation of the Holy Spirit. Without that relationship the church, no matter how successful or economically strong, it will die.

This time, another protestant church's Pastor, who did not like seeing that some of his own members had come to my meetings, started the opposition.

He began by entreating them to stay away and exhorted them to stop attending our meetings. In a letter to the congregation he warned them their attendance was dangerous to their souls. His exhortations made them more inclined to attend our services, and they began to take their evangelistic duties more seriously, telling others of the joy they experienced in worship and studying with us.

Lastly he went to the governor of the city. He did his best by saying:

"You should get rid of this new teaching before it gets much worse. They are spoiling the youth and convincing them to keep Saturday just like the Jews. We Christians keep Sunday for our worship. He is leading them into a new and heretical sect of the Jews. Some are citizens from Karak itself and the man who instructs them is called Najeeb Azar."

The Mayor said, "If that man belongs to the Azars of Jordan which is considered a good family with a good record in the kingdom, he cannot be a Jew. I know they are Christians."

The Pastor replied, "Yes they are, though he follows the Jews and goes by the Old Testament."

"I also know about that, said the Mayor, they must have a good reason for that if they believe it is right to keep Saturday as the Sabbath. I'll call that minister you mentioned and ask him about it."

"But now, tell me," continued the Mayor, "you are Christian aren't you, why are you opposing others who also profess to be Christians? I do not see how it can be good behavior for a Pastor of Christ to be persecuting others just because they differ in some principals of their faith."

After that the Governor/Mayor called me and asked many questions concerning my faith. The meeting with him was strange and encouraging. I do not know if all that he heard created a new found faith in him, but I do know that we became good friends. We talked for one and a half hours that day.

"Go on, he said, with our blessings. Yours is the best Christian set of principals and actions I have come to know about and it is the closest to Islam. I will help you all that I can. And make sure that nobody will be able to hurt you."

After that I purposefully sought out the offending pastor and befriended him. We did become friends, his faith and my own were broadened by the experience and we worked together to bring welfare to the youth of our region. And much spiritual fruit was harvested as a result of our cooperation.

My wife was teaching in the Karak School. There were family activities for the youth. Both the Church and the School were conducted as social instruments. There were gatherings and games, both indoors and outdoors, helping us become a more community oriented center for the local families. We had picnics as a school and a church. We invited everyone. More and more people came to both of them, and in so doing we had more and more friends, brothers and sisters with whom to conduct Gods work. My mother came to stay with us. We needed her, and she felt at home with us. She and my wife got along very nicely as mother and daughter.

That year the Lord blessed us with our first baby. We received a gift from heaven. It is a great time for the family to gain knowledge in knowing God as a loving Father, also to appreciate one another as husband and wife. Parents do their very best to keep their child away from harm and hurtful distractions.

Again it puzzles man's human thinking to think of God, as having one son whom He loved so dearly, and yet that he might allow the sacrifice of that beautiful Son to save such people like us.

This entire theological difficulty, the willingness of the Father to sacrifice His Son for me and mine and you and yours, however, it befuddles me to consider how much it strengthens me and my family. As we live together in the knowledge that it is His love and Sacrifice alone that have provided this promise of joy for us all.

The day our first child was born (November l4th, 1955) two hundred and fifty men and women came to congratulate us. They were all happy that we had been blessed with Gods' good favor in giving us a boy child, a son as our first baby. Our firstborn would be the bearer of our family name. Our daughters would come, and grow and we would love them dearly and forever but when they leave us to go to their husbands' homes, they would then become a blessing to that family having sons and daughters who would bear that family's name forward. And for us, should we have more sons, the more to carry our name forward. In times of difficulty, in times of need those families, created through the bearing of the name forward become a great instrument of healing for the entire family.

More people were coming to both the church services and sending their children to our church school. A pastor is expected to be on duty 24 hours a day, seven days a week. Anytime he would be called should respond and help. A visit to a sick person may be requested any hour of the day or night. A prayer cannot be accepted over the phone. He has to go, read, encourage and pray. He might be asked to take that patient to a physician or hospital.

I assumed those responsibilities taking it after my father whom I loved so much. In fact I gave my father's name to my son. Victor means Naser in Arabic – considering my father a Victor, the way he lived. The way he was converted, he gave up smoking and drinking alcohol and showed more love to his wife and children. In the church, pastor's absence, he would take his place as a preacher. His sermons were beautiful and rich with his personal experiences. Many would come to listen. He was the only staff for the school that he started. Both Christian and Moslem children were admitted to that old fashioned school. If Jesus would accept everybody, my father would accept everybody too.

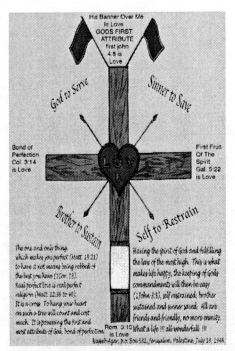

This was a chart that Najeeb created while living in Jerusalem in the year 1946.

Najeeb Azar posing with his wife Najla.

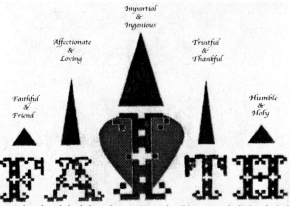

Impartial & Ingenious

Affectionate & Loving

Trustful & Thankful

Faithful & Friend

Humble & Holy

Nobody lives without it. To have the right kind of it, and to have it complete means living well. It is yours as long as it is in your heart. To be sure that it is there, you should have it. If not, you will not have it. The moment you endeavor to show it, it disappears. When you open your hands, it flies. It should be seen without being shown. If you try to earn it you will lose it. If you needed and wanted it and were too poor, you will have it. It is a gift from God and God grants it through the hearing and reading of his word.

His words will keep you in faith if you by faith and faithfully keep them. For "F", we become faithful and friendly. For "A", we become affectionate and loving. With "I", we become impartial and ingenious. With "T", we are always trustful and thankful. The "H" will bring us lastly humility and holiness. Behold my hands and follow me says Jesus.

Najeeb Azar, Beit Jala, Palestine, 1946.

This was another expression of Najeeb's faith, which he created also in 1946 in Beit Jala near Jerusalem. This chart was made when Najeeb met with Dr. Moses who claimed to be the messiah.

Najla is posing here for this photo, after her engagement to Najeeb Azar at her parent's house in northern Jordan. From this porch the Golan Heights as well as Mount Hermon in Lebanon can be seen.

Naser Azar (Najeeb's Father) on the right and a Seventh Day Adventist preacher in Jordan.

Najla and Najeeb's Cousin preparing the grapes to make wine.

Najla and her brother Fo'ad near one of the cedars of Lebanon in Mount Lebanon.

My father-In-Law, Najla's Father, Milad Elaimy is with traditional clothing.

Najla is on a ski lift on Mount Lebanon.

Najeeb & Najla Azar's are getting married at the Amman Seventh Day Adventist Church in Jordan. This was the first wedding to be performed at this brand new church in 1954.

Najeeb & Najla's are at their Wedding.

The newlyweds, Najeeb and Najla

Najla at the Wedding.

Pictured here, from left to right are Najla's nephew Hani Nimri, Najla's sister Basima, Najla's Father Milad, Najla's Mother Hana, Najla's Brother Fo'ad, Najla, Najeeb, Najeeb's brother George, Najeeb's Mother Katrina, Najla's brother-in-law Suliman, Najla's sister Badi'a holding her baby Hanan. In the front row, from left to right are Badi'a's daughter Evlyn and, squatting, Najeeb's brother wadi.

In the doorway behind the students are Najla and Najeeb's nephew Saleh, the teachers of the new church school in Karak Jordan.

This is the second year of the school in Karak where there are more students. Najla stands behind the students.

Najeeb is shown here holding his son Victor and standing next to Najla. This picture was taken in Ghor El safi in the Jordan Valley south of the Dead Sea. This location is close to where the cities of Sodom and Gommorah are said to have existed.

The Azars are with Najeeb's Mother Katrina.

Victor and Viola in Ramallah, Palestine.

The Azars after baby Viola was born

The Azars in Ramallah where Najeeb is holding their daughter Viola, Najla in standing behind Najeeb and Katrina is next to Najeeb. Najeeb's brother wadi is holding his son Naser and behind him is his wife holding their daughter Kawther. Victor is standing in front.

The Azars after the first baby Katy was born. This Katy passed away in Jerusalem two years later.

Najla and a family friend in traditional Palestinian dress.

In Baghdad, Iraq at Najla's brother Foad's house.

The Azars are in Jerusalem in their house on the Mount of Olives with some of the church members.

The Azars kids with friends in Basra, Iraq, after the second Katy was born who is sitting between Viola and Victor.

Picnic with friends under the palm trees in Basra

Here, the Azars are with the closest friends the Murad family and the Abu Qais family in Basra

Boy scout and Girl Scout, Victor and Viola with Katy standing in between.

At the new church in Basra with the Murad family

This is the Seventh Day Adventist church in Baghdad.

*In the home town of El-Husn in Northern
Jordan at Najla's parents garden.*

Victor and Viola with Dad

Samer, the youngest of the Azar's children was also born in Basra

The Azars near the Iraq/Kuwait border

The Azars are standing near Najeeb's first car a Volkswagen while at the Habbaniah Lake near Baghdad.

At the Habbaniah Lake with church friends.

The Azar children in El Husn in Northers Jordan

Having dinner at Najeeb's in-laws in El Husn.

Witnessing To Moslems

Two years were spent in the blessedness of hard work with and for the Lord in Karak. I still remember one of those nights when two very important Moslem leaders came to visit me. One of them headed the Islamic Brotherhood Association in Jordan. He was an extremely fanatic Moslem. The other man was a leading personality in his own Moslem family, a very powerful and respected tribe.

"We have come to you, Pastor, to ask you some questions about Christianity as a whole and about your faith as a Christian", one of them started.

"Why have you come to me instead of going to some other Christian leaders?"

"We did, but are not satisfied with their answers, so we come to you because we were told that you knew your religion very well"

"Yes, by the grace of God, I know my bible and I study it everyday. Do I understand that you want straight answers to your questions"

"That is what we want please"

"Would we consider that we are brothers with no intentions of hurting or offending one another, so that I am allowed to be sincere and frank?"

Many Christians lack the courage to testify to their faith. They fail to do it with love taking it for granted that those seeking the light would be saved eternally. How could we withhold the light from people resulting in their eternal loss!

That night we had some rules to go by. It is so hard to be as wise as serpents and as meek as doves. All of these questions directed to me were answered directly and frankly. Four hours were spent that night. The first question was: We have come to find the real Gospel. I directed them to the Bible, which was placed on the table, and said all the Gospels are in this book, the Holy Bible. They said no, we want to know about the missing one. I said, how did you know there was a missing Gospel? You are Moslems, why do care about that. I will tell you why you are asking about the missing Gospel.

"Yes pastor, tell us"

"While you were reading your holy Koran, you were told that the Torah is with the Jews and the Gospels are with the Christians. So the Koran told you that the Christians have the Gospels. I am a Christian, so you came to the right place to look for it".

"You are right. So what is your answer?"

"Since I am a Christian and I'm telling you that this is the Gospel and there is nothing missing, you have to believe me, if you believe in your own Koran."

"Yes, we believe it is the Gospel, in the hand of you the Christian, but now who is Issa (Jesus in Arabic) and what relationship does he have with God?"

I looked at one of them and asked him, "If I want to know who you are, whom should I ask?"

He said, "Ask me, because I know the best about myself".

Then I said, " You are right, so to know who Jesus or Issa is, we should ask him about who he is".

"In the Gospels, he refers to himself as the Son of God and many other names, as you can read."

"But God does not have a Son, he did not get married".

I said, "It is not necessary that God should be married in order to have children. Don't we, humans have children whom we adopt?"

They said, "So God adopted Issa"

I said that the Koran says that he put his spirit into Miriam (Mary), while she was a virgin to give birth to Jesus. So it was a super natural birth. Nobody was born like him. The Koran says that Satan stung everyone born of a woman, except Issa the son of Mary. This means that everybody is a sinner, including all the prophets except for Jesus.

They asked, "what else can you tell us about Jesus?"

I said do you remember that the Koran says Issa is going to be the Judge of the world?

They said, yes the Koran says so. Then they asked, what is the difference between the Bible and the Koran? And what do you think about the Prophet Mohammad.

There are some differences I said, for example, the Koran says that God created Jesus the same way he created Adam from the earth. In another verse, it says that God sent his spirit to Miriam. There are contradictions in the Koran. In another verse, you are limited to four wives in this life, while in another verse God will give seventy-two virgins to the least believer. Why are you limited here and given that many there. Also, you are forbidden to drink wine here, while in heaven you will be given a river of wine to enjoy day and night. There are many contradictions in the Koran.

They said, "What do you think of the prophet Mohammad?"

I said, "He was a very wise man to convert the heathen Arabs to God and to unite them and to give them purpose. To control them in this life, he promised them better things in the afterlife. The Prophet Mohammad did not want his followers to indulge in too many women or be drunk all the time because he wanted them to complete his mission on this earth.

After the four hour meeting with them, one of them said, I believe in our Master Issa (Jesus). The other one said, May God not let me die except as a believer in Issa.

My wife was praying in the other room for my safety. She was happy that the visitors did not harm me.

To Ramallah (The West Bank Of The Jordan)

Both Church and school were well organized and that could be a sign that movements or transfers would happen in the organization. The mission board met to discuss such topics. The west bank of Jordan had some difficulties in church growth. The board thought to exchange workers. The pastor in the west bank was named to replace me in Karak. To do that, I should be moved to the west bank to be in charge of Jerusalem, Ramallah (which means "the City of God") and Bethlehem. At first, we lived in Ramallah, five miles north of Jerusalem.

Our second child, a girl who was born in Karak, whom we named Viola, was eighteen days old when we obeyed the call of the Lord to move to Ramallah. We were very happy to have Viola, as did all of our friends. Our customs demand that a woman should stay at home for forty days after delivery. She is not supposed to even go to church. Though in our case, we could not wait that long. Rammallah was the place chosen for us to live in. It is located to the northwest of Jerusalem. It was one of the most beautiful places in Palestine. It was also a summer resort because of its beauty and moderate weather. It was in this city that our third child was born whom we named Katy, after the name of my mother Katrina.

There was no church or church school for our mission in Ramallah. So we started some primary activities, visitations and encouraging former church members that we usually classify as apostatizers to come back and worship with us. As for outsiders, very few cared for religion.

In Ramallah, we had a well-devoted member who was the first baptized man in Palestine. That man was a real help through his example and zeal. He often would join me in visitations. My wife was very supportive, encouraging and helped me with the visitations also.

Persecution In Palestine

As the work grew and more people showed interest to join the church, word reached the governor of Jerusalem warning him against us. This Governor was in charge of the whole west bank including Ramallah. Many false accusations were made. The Governor refused to discuss the accusations with me and ordered my family and I to pack up and leave Jerusalem in twenty-four hours. Which is what we did. The West Bank was then under the Hashemite Kingdom of Jordan. In effect, we were thrown out of our own country. This was very strange.

In Amman, the capital of Jordan, I protested to the Government, and in a short time I was permitted back with my family into Jerusalem and the West Bank.

Moving from Ramallah to Jerusalem

Two years later, a German pastor accepted a call to come to Jerusalem. I was asked to move to Jerusalem to assist him because he did not know the Arabic language. We rented two apartments next to each other for both his family and mine. Since there was no church building for us in Jerusalem, our apartment, which was located on the Mount of Olives overlooking the old city, was used for church services. We had a great feeling living on the Mount of Olives where Jesus ascended to heaven.

During that time, in Jerusalem, our daughter Katy, who was Eighteen months old, got sick with diphtheria and passed away. We buried her in Jerusalem near the Golden Gate.

To Basra, Iraq

In the later part of 1960, I was called again to serve in my hometown. That was the third time that I was serving in my hometown Al-Husn, this time we expected to stay there at least five years. We needed to relax and not be moved again as rapidly as we did so far. Our services were needed here in the north district of Jordan as a whole.

Just before that transfer, I was ordained for the Gospel ministry, which took place in Beirut, Lebanon on November 24, 1960. My wife was standing by me.

On the day of ordination, I received a call to work in Basra, Iraq. That was one thousand miles east of Jordan. Basra itself is fifty miles east of Qornah, where both the great Tigris and Euphrates rivers meet to form a much larger river on which Basra is located. Qornah, is where the Tree of the knowledge of Good and Evil was located in Adam's days according to local Islamic legend. It is also believed that the Garden of Eden was there. The locals there point to a dead tree stump and a sign next to it that says that our Father Abraham stopped while he was on his way from Ur, just south of that point before he continued on his way to Canaan. Abraham is said to have worshiped thrice at the stump. Worshiping three times signifies a Moslem way of worship. Therefore according to Islamic tradition, Abraham was Moslem, although Islam did not exist at that time.

In the Basra area we were told later that there were about thirty kinds of dates, and over thirty million palm trees. We used to eat fresh dates there and were able to distinguish between the different kinds. It was great to work in that beautiful city. Having just been ordained,

I thought that it was an obligation to accept that call. Again, I didn't think that it was right to do so without discussing it with my wife. She was always my best help and therefore, she should have the right to join me in making decisions. I carried the news to her, and both of us discussed the matter and took it to the Lord in prayer.

Later we had some questions for the Mission president, such as "isn't it too hot for our children there?", "yes, it is" he said, "but you know there are many people living there already".

Another question we had was "couldn't any Iraqi minister be given that post in his own country, one who knows his own people's ways, customs, and culture?" He said "there is already one there and we want someone else to replace him". Another question we asked was "What are we expected to do there that would be different to warrant my family and myself to move all the way there?"

He said, "We want you to do the work of a minister, to visit, study, and pray with the few members left there. We want you to work towards building a real good and beautiful church in Basra. You are the man for that city".

We asked another question, "Am I not wanted where I am located now in my hometown?" I always believed in asking questions. He said, "yes you are wanted here in Jordan and you are wanted for Basra. However, you are needed more in Basra.

Our stay at Al-Husn was only five months. In the fall of 1961, we packed and headed towards Basra.

In Basra it took us four months to get adjusted to the Iraqi culture. We also had to get used to the special dialect that they spoke with. Although they spoke the Arabic language, it seemed to us like it was a different language all together. Being so close to Iran, there was a lot of influence from the Farsi language. There were influences from other languages too, such as English (because of the WW1 British mandate over Iraq), Kurdish (because of the presence of many Kurds there), and Assyrian (the original indigenous Christians of Iraq). It was interesting and in time became enjoyable.

It was very hard for us having nobody to show us around to acquaint us with the church members or the town in general. We felt very lost. It seemed that no other minister wanted to be there and we were the ones to be banished into this God forsaken area of the world.

We started advertising the lots of land that the church owned to sell them since they were not in a suitable zone to build a church on. We were advised to sell them and buy one good lot of land in a good area for that project. We completed eleven month working there in selling and buying land.

While in Basra, our children were so often exposed to colds and other illnesses they ran extremely high fevers that were beyond our control. Our next-door neighbor Doctor Afram was so kind and helpful whenever needed. We never forget his kindness. He always made sure that we never hesitate to call him any time for help. Though the fact that he never charged us for his checkups and medicines, was too much for us to take. We found out later that doctors and midwives never charge clergymen, regardless of denomination or religion.

On one occasion as our daughter Viola ran a very high fever, we took her to another doctor who gave her some kind of medicine that he thought would be good for her. We did not go to our neighbor, the doctor, this time because we were too embarrassed to take advantage of him knowing that he would not take our money no matter what. Though, after we gave her the other doctor's medicine, her fever became worst. So, in the afternoon, we took her to our neighbor. As he saw those pills, he was extremely angry. When we asked him why he was angry, he said that if we had given Viola one more tablet, it would have killed her. He took those tablets, dumped them and gave her a different medicine that took her fever away.

The thought struck me then, why would some doctors not give the right medicine! Was it the same reason mentioned in the Holy Bible? I remembered the story of the lady who bled for twelve years. The Gospel's record tells that she did not suffer from the disease itself but rather from many physicians. Some of those who chose to take such a sacred responsibility to relieve and help people were not concerned for the welfare of their patients but rather to get the most money possible. They forget that their task is heavenly appointed. Take this medicine they say. Try it for two weeks and come back for another checkup. Either they lack knowledge or they do not intend to relieve their patients the quickest way possible, giving medicine on guessing basis, resulting in weakening the body and destroying other parts of the body which were not involved with the disease.

I remember once when we lived in Ramallah, my doctor prescribed medicine for my stomach, while my pain was in my back. I protested because my digestion was good and I had no pains in my stomach. "Never mind," he said, but sometimes stomach diseases cause headaches. I did not buy that prescription. If physicians were faithful to their sacred calling and are honest with their patients, this would be a better world.

To Baghdad

The Iraqi mission president made a phone call to me one of those nights telling me to move at once to Baghdad.

"You sure don't mean it, brother Behnam" I said, "we have not been here long enough to complete the project we came for". He said, "yes, I mean it, the committee here took an action to have you pastor the church in Baghdad. We expect you to come right away, find yourself a house, and then bring your family over". Then I asked, "For how long would I stay in Baghdad". He Said, "Forever".

That phone call was made after midnight. The next morning, I flew to Baghdad. In two days, I rented a house, which later proved not satisfactory to my wife. After moving to that house, my wife found a more suitable house to live in.

As I told my wife of the committee's action to serve in the Baghdad church, she did not object because she thought that it was going to be forever this time. The fact that her brother lived in Baghdad was also part of why she was happy with the decision. Baghdad is also home of one of the largest and most affluent church communities in the Middle East. Our community there also owned a hospital and a school for our children. Therefore, being the pastor of that church would be a very positive move for my career. We moved there at the end of 1962.

In the course of the eleven months that we spent in Baghdad, a very bloody civil war happened. They called such civil wars "revolutions". This is when one regime replaces another. Which scared us to death several times. One night during that war, an armored car full of soldiers came to our neighbors' house and arrested the man who was the Interior Minister of the old regime. We heard later that he died in prison.

While still in Baghdad, the division president came to visit Iraq. That particular division in our church encompassed North Africa and the Middle East. When he saw that I was the pastor in Baghdad, he was surprised and he insisted that I should go back to Basra to continue my project there. This was not good news to my wife; however, she accepted that decision. We moved again to Basra.

One of the hardships that we had to always face was our children's schooling. Most of the time we were not able to be in an area where there are church schools. They had to attend public or private schools. The problem with this is that in the Middle East, the Moslems have Fridays off for worship and the Christians have Their Sundays off. Therefore, the public schools there are usually off on Friday and the private schools were off on Fridays and Sundays. We as Seventh Day Adventists keep Saturday as the Sabbath. So to enroll our children in those schools, we had to work very had to convince the Principles in these schools to let our children have Saturdays off. They usually asked questions about whether we were Jews. Being a Jew (which is not what we are) is not a good thing in the Arab world. The Jews are their enemies and were looked down upon. To be accepted and admitted, our children had to get special attention from the teachers and from us the parents on the missing lessons that other children got on Saturday. The teachers also were resentful because they had to do extra work. Additionally, our children were always persecuted and teased by the other children who used to call them Jews, they would ask again and again about the reason for their absence every Saturday. We had to always coach our children about reasons why they are going through all of this. It was not healthy for our children to be mocked continuously. We would always tell them that we are God's chosen people and that God's people always face persecution. Our children's lives were a continuous pain and struggle.

Construction started on the planned church on the lot we already purchased in one of the best areas of Basra. The funding for this church came from the affluent members of the Baghdad Church. It was designed to look like a Cathedral with long arched stained glass windows and living quarters for the minister and his family as well as a guesthouse. I remember that a stained glass artist was brought in from Italy for that purpose. When it was finished it was thought to be the most beautiful church in the Middle East. Photographers used to come from all over to take pictures of it. We also noticed artists set up their easels to paint their impressions of the church. We had even imported a Grand Piano, which was the only one of its kind in the area.

Visitations were started at the same time as the start of the construction. We wanted to prepare the members for the dedication service. We invited some local government, army and police officials as well. The Governor of Basra was invited and became a good friend of mine. We also invited the heads of the other denominations including the Bishop of the Anglican Church who used to come and worship with us even before the church was dedicated. The prayer that he offered was an old fashioned powerful prayer with both his hands lifted upwards.

Many were happy that the church was built. The dedication was well attended by many who came from Basra, Baghdad and Beirut, Lebanon. The general conference president from the United States came to lead the Service. They had me serve as the interpreter. The night that it was dedicated, it was more than full and everybody was happy.

Arrested By The Iraqi Secret Police

To build a church, money is needed. That money had to be raised locally, otherwise it would be suspected as a foreign project financed by America. Local people should sponsor it. Those motives behind building a church would be questioned. Why build a big beautiful church for five members. That's all we had in Basra. Suspicions arose. It was one of those Saturday mornings as I was preaching in the church that two policemen were sent to arrest me. The government as well as the Moslem religious laws did not allow them to arrest a minister while preaching. So they waited outside until the service was completed.

As I was greeting the people at the door coming out of the sanctuary one of the policemen said "good morning sir, excuse me but we are ordered to arrest you and take you to the police head officer". They were on foot, so I asked them "shall we take my car?" They looked at each other and one of them said, "what a good man he is". They then insisted on walking and decided not to handcuff me. "The police station is nearby," they said.

That event was preceded by a similar event. Others were arrested, one of whom I knew. Before they had the opportunity to defend themselves, they were executed by hanging. For me, even though I was a foreigner it was still dangerous.

As far as parties working politically against the government trying to overthrow it, it was necessary for those officials to investigate as well as prevent any activities that would threaten the ruling regime. They wanted to do their best to make it enjoyable for people to live there. That's what I felt. As I was admitted into that mysterious and dangerous office, the officer started, "Are you Najeeb Azar, the Jordanian?" "Yes Sir," I said. And do you own a blue Volkswagen car with the license plate - 174n Baghdad? – Do you know that you are being watched by us day and night and we know where you go and where you park your car?" I said, "I should be thankful for that sir. This is very kind and generous of you, I feel honored and protected." My response surprised him and he smiled and I felt happy and refreshed. I was told to sit down. He said that they were aware of my repeated visits to a particular lady and he said what would be the reason for these visits. I told him that my job as a minister is to visit the church members at home.

He asked about what the visits would be about. I told him that I read from God's holy book and answer her questions and pray for her. He asked about why that is important. I told him that people needed to be taught and encouraged in life. He said that he thought that Christians went to Church and did not need to be taught or visited. I said that not every Christian by birth is Christian in deed and those who do not follow Christ, how could they by right claim his name. He was puzzled and I continued, I mean that a Christian in deed should live a righteous life, does not follow the world's bad habits and practices. A Christian would not be among those who would drink, gamble, smoke, curse, etc. He said that his understanding of Christians is that they are allowed to indulge in all of these habits, and wondered if according to me that those Christians are really Christians. I said to him that judgment belongs to God and those who follow Him should apply the Gospel.

The officer at this point was wondering why would a Jordanian come to Iraq to advise people how to live. He wondered if Jordanians have better Christian standards than Iraqis. I told him that the Jordanians did not reach perfection and no one in the world could ever attain that. As for me being here in Iraq, I told him, that I was invited by the Iraqi church members to perform my pastoral duties in their country. I really don't feel that I am a stranger among the wonderful Iraqi people. He then wondered if no one can attain perfection, then what would be the point. I then continued that we all are alike being the children of Adam and Eve. We are apt to fall and fail. Though a Christian is taught by God's holy book to ever strive towards perfection and keep away from sin or transgression. God promised to help people when they are that sincere.

He then became interested in the differences between my denomination and the other Christian denominations. I explained that all Christians have the same Bible as a resource. Some endeavor to apply its teaching more than others. Understanding the Bible is very important because our faith is built on the way we understand our book. He asked if there was more than one way to understand the Bible? I told him that there is only one way to understand the Bible. We read in it that getting drunk keeps people away from heaven and eternal life so we do not use alcoholic beverages. Also, the creator, for reasons sometimes unknown in the book itself, prohibited eating pork. Some people take such an advise literally while others don't. We also don't smoke because we consider our bodies God's property and should be kept clean. He was impressed and asked why we build a huge and expensive church for only a handful of followers. I explained that we don't have many followers but they deserve to worship God in a beautiful church. In fact, this church is not ours. It is rather God's house of worship for anyone who desires to worship him. He asked if he as a Moslem could worship God the way he wants in the church. I told him that he could surely do that and that we will open the door for him anytime he wants.

Next, the officer wanted to know where did the funding came from to build the church. I told him that this organization considers itself one worldwide family. We received no funding from any government in the world. All believers give liberally for the cause. This church was built from such sources. The officer was impressed and said that we were the best Christian church to his knowledge. That visit took almost two hours and ended with a real good friendship.

Building a beautiful church with a house attached to it for the pastor, a guesthouse and a huge yard turned into a lovely flower garden and a fancy fence was built around the complex aroused the suspicion in those who ignored the motives of those who built and those who sponsored. The church pastor would be the only one called for investigation. That day that I was called to appear at the intelligence office in Basra, everyone gazed at me. Only political criminals would be brought over there. That was a mysterious room full of scary instruments. The officer who sat there was very kind and gentle. I was greeted with a smile. His questions though were of the same sort as those that would cause me to tremble before I could think of any answers. Though somehow as a minister of God, I felt that I don't have to worry, especially that I knew that I did not have anything to fear. On the other hand, if God wants to be glorified by my martyrdom, I would welcome it. I had nothing to do with politics, nor did I work against any government or religion. So I thought to give it a smile and go on.

The intelligence officer said that he asked me to come and give him straight answers to his questions. He told me to relax and not be afraid. I told him that I knew where I stand and how my stance is so mysterious. I also know that I am surrounded with fearful instruments that every movement and every word is recorded. I also know that I have nothing to be afraid of or to be ashamed of and that I am aware that he is a good man doing his best to serve his country as best he can. I told him that I was ready for his questions.

He said that some people suspect me to be a Jew working for Jewish interests and he wanted to know if this was true. I told him that I was a Christian and had nothing to do with the Jews. The only common thing that I had with the Jews is that I keep Saturday for a Sabbath. He asked why would a Christian pray on Saturday? I told him that if God gave the same commandment to both the Jews and the Moslems, would the Moslems refuse to obey God in order to not be associated with the Jews? He said no, however, he wanted to know which commandment I meant. I said there are some commandments that prohibit the Jews as well as the Moslems from eating pork. Another commandment that is shared between the Jews and the Moslems is circumcision. We, too, as Seventh Day Adventists do not eat pork in keeping with the same commandment. He agreed and wanted to know more about the Saturday question. I said that it is God's commandment, which is mentioned in your Koran as one of God's ten words. He then said that Saturday was not one of them. I insisted that it was mentioned in the Koran, which says that God turned those Jews who did not observe it into monkeys. Satisfied with my answer, he wanted to know more about other doctrines that we have that other Christians do not have. I said that according to the Bible, the only Christian resource, we do not drink alcoholic beverages, smoke or eat pork like other Christians do. Another doctrine is that some Christians pay tithes to support God's work. This is much like your religion with the doctrine of Zakat where you give five percent of your income. He wanted to know what would happen if the tithes are not spent correctly for God's work. I said then the tithes should not be given to the church but rather to the poor. Our people's eyes are open in that respect. He wondered if our preaching with such doctrines would be dangerous to other Christian denominations in Basra. I said I wish they could. He was shocked and asked what I meant. Instead of answering the question, I asked him, if he had a truth that he believed in and was moved by it, would he want to be vindicated and testify for the truth or would he keep silent. He asked if I would still preach the truth if it would hurt others. I told him, that I would not hurt any one and that the other churches would not be affected or offended. Again, he wanted me to explain what I meant. I said that to become good Christians, a man should stop hurting himself, others and his God. Good Christians do not abuse their bodies with alcohol, cigarettes and harmful foods. Good Christians honor God and follow his ten words, which include no adultery, no steeling, and the rest of God's words. Then he said that we would not be a danger of taking away a large portion of other denomination's memberships because it is very hard to follow my churches doctrine. I agreed, though I told him that it is my desire that everyone would follow God the best they can, then we would lead a most wonderful life as brothers.

As a result, we became friends and I was registered as the church representative and one of the dignitaries of the city. I started to receive invitations to official functions and different occasions. I was grateful that God gave me favor and grace with those in authority in Iraq. During the last year of our stay in Iraq, I had no troubles with the authorities in Basra and was considered as one of their own.

During that time the president of Iraq came to visit Basra for a whole week to gain the favor of the tribes in that city. There were many celebrations and ribbon cutting ceremonies that I was invited to join the entourage of the president along with the other dignitaries and the heads of the tribes. It seemed that every breakfast, lunch and dinner were spent with president Abdul Salam Aref.

On the last evening of his visit to Basra, I was invited along with the same group to have dinner with him at the Basra airport. We were waiting for him to arrive by helicopter from Qornah (mentioned above as the traditional Garden of Eden, according to Islamic tradition) to have dinner with him. We waited for a long time and something felt bad about the situation. Some of the Guards and officials were behaving in a strange way. Then the Governor's secretary invited everyone to eat without the president being there.

We found out the next morning that he was assassinated with the ten ministers as well as the Governor of Basra.

The Six-Day War

The last two years of our stay in Basra, calls had been coming to go back to serve in my country, Jordan. There was a shortage of ministers there. They wanted a minister to take charge in northern Jordan where there were two churches and a church school. Those calls never reached me. We were wanted in Basra as well.

In the course of those two years, our children's education was getting more difficult. We hoped a call would come for us to go to some country where there would be a church school.

The third call of 1967 was given to me with the hope that we would refuse it. In spite of the fact that we were well appreciated there, yet there was a good reason for us to accept the call. In a few days, I got my wife and children ready and sent them by plane to Amman, Jordan. I had to stay another 45 days until another preacher came and took over.

A wife is well and much more appreciated when her husband has to stay alone that long. Cooking, doing kitchen work and taking care of his cleaning. On top of that, preparing for church work and visitation. I felt lost without my family. I could hardly wait until the man who replaced me came. I spent some time with him to get him acquainted with people and places. No one did that for me when I got to Basra.

After my obligations were done, I was ready to go to Jordan. I rented a truck and loaded it with our belongings and started home. Letters from my wife told me that she already rented a house for us in Irbid. The address of that house was given in one of those letters. It was on June, 3, 1967 that I was on my way by truck riding next to the driver coming from Basra to Jordan. During the day when we were on the Baghdad-Amman highway, the Iraqi troops along with their armored cars and tanks were on their way to enter Jordan. This was done according to a joint defense agreement that Iraq joined which included Jordan, Egypt and Syria. They intended to join the rest of the Arabs against the Jews in that year's war. Traveling along side the army is dangerous during a time of war. In fact, I was miraculously saved on that trip because of the bombing that occurred on that highway. The Israeli air force jets were raiding the Iraqi Army all around us. We saw much death and destruction. That was a horrifying scary experience.

On June 4th, I arrived in Irbid and unloaded the furniture in our new house. With our belongings, I had a beautiful hand made Persian carpet, which I could hardly get out of Iraq. It was considered as money and money was not allowed out of Iraq. I had to argue with the customs manager to let me keep it. I told him that I wanted to have something beautiful to remind me of Iraq. We intended to unpack the next morning. When the morning came, news June 5th broke out between the Arab and the Jews. This is the famous 6 day war which resulted in the Arabs losing the West bank, including Jerusalem, Gaza, Sinai, and the Golan Heights. We had to flee from Irbid to Al-Husn, our home town and we left our belongings unpacked.

Irbid was closer to the Golan Heights and was bombed continuously by Israel. We stayed in Al-Husn until there was no more danger in going back to Irbid.

Eze 8:1, was taken to have been meant as an old-testament prophecy fulfilled at that time. It read, "on the fifth day of the sixth month". Everybody thought that it was fulfilled in that war which then took place. I was asked several times whether that verse had any baring on that present day's event. The narration from the eighth chapter of Ezekiel does not fit those happenings. Any text misunderstood would scare the people of the Holy Land and make them believe that it might be the hand of God working for the good of one party against the other.

It takes quite an effort to convince people of the righteousness of God, that He does not discriminate against any peoples or takes sides. Taking the west bank from Jordan, Sinai from Egypt and the Golan Heights from Syria added to the problem of the refugees. These Palestinian refugees either ran away for their lives or were driven away from their homes and properties. We used to see them walking barefooted across the borders into the fields of what was left of Jordan. They settled in the nearest countries that they were able to walk to, namely Jordan and Syria.

It was a tragedy and heartbreaking to watch those thousands denied life as it were, most of them as they left had no more than their clothing. They had to rush forgetting what to take or what to leave. It is related about a lady that instead of carrying her child in her flight on reaching Jordan found out that what she carried was a pillow, not her child. Many similar stories were being told.

There were insufficient resources in Jordan for the refugees. That created many problems. Jordanians opened their homes and were very generous to the refugees in need of help. It was felt an obligation to sacrifice for them. In time, efforts were organized by the United Nations and different organizations from around the world to send tents and erect camps for these refugees. Food supplies, medicine and clothing were also provided. These supplies were restricted to only the refugees, while the Jordanians who were poor and were affected by the war were neglected. These camps with the overcrowded conditions and poor living standards still exist until now.

Our church was to distribute food, bedding, medicine and clothing that was sent in by the mission and I was in charge of the distribution. It took me much effort and persuasion to get the authorities to allow me to distribute some of the supplies to the poor and the affected, regardless of whether they were refugees, indigenous Jordanians, Moslems or Christians.

Some were able to get jobs and improve their condition and move out of the camps into the cities, build homes and live in them. Some were able to start businesses and soon were well to do. These people are a minority; most of the refugees are still refugees and depend on the welfare of the United Nations.

Match Making

The pastor I used to visit in Karak, who was from a different denomination, was transferred to Irbid, Jordan. It was a pleasant surprise to see him there again. He had much better feelings towards us than he had in Karak. We became very close friends. I hired his daughter, Nouha, to teach in our school in Irbid. Later, Nouha became interested in one of our ministers. The way Bishara, our minister, wanted to propose to her, was the old traditional way that it is done in Jordan. He asked for my help. I agreed to help, knowing that she is a good girl and will be a good wife for him. Bishara, used to be the minister of another city in Jordan. He is originally a Palestinian from Jerusalem. The only correct way to help him was to take him to the girl's parents and there we would ask them for her hand. According to tradition, the parents should agree first, and then, would consult the girl's opinion. The night that we went to them to propose, we intended to make sure that they would agree to that marriage. Since both their daughter and Bishara loved each other, and we thought that it was a good match. The clergyman's word, that is I, was well appreciated and his advice would be accepted.

According to the custom, coffee is served before the proposal is made. On the other hand, coffee will not be had before the proposal was accepted. Those parents were expected to accept to give their daughter hand in marriage upon her agreement, if they wanted the proposing party to drink their coffee. It is usually a shame to a host to have a visitor reject their coffee. Usually though, nobody such as my self being the minister, would get involved unless he is certain that his request would be accepted. Therefore I had to do some homework before hand to insure a positive result. The reason that I was doing the proposing is because Bishara was expected by tradition to get someone as myself to propose on his behalf.

Coffee was served. My wife, Bishara and myself took our cups and laid them on the table and I started to speak. I said, "We consider it a great pleasure to visit you, though we have come with a purpose in mind and we trust that you would not turn us away. Brother Bishara would like to have the honor of becoming your son-in-law, he is asking for Nouha's hand in marriage. What is your answer? Upon your acceptance, we will drink your coffee." Nouha's father with a humorous spirit looked at me and said jokingly "ha ha, have you started taking my family one after the other?" My good friend meant that I was converting his family to my church away from his. I said, "yes, but I would not be satisfied without you getting in as well." He said, "do you really think that I am still outside the church? I am an Adventist before you." (Years later he joined the church too.) I pressed for an answer and he said "consider my daughter yours. We accept the proposal, please drink your coffee and we will ask Nouha about her opinion." We had already known through Bishara that she would accept, so we drank the coffee.

Terrorism
Trouble in the north

When the Israelis captured the West bank from Jordan, the Gaza Strip from Egypt and the Golan heights from Syria, the Palestinians, with the help of Russia and China, started to form groups and train them for operations against the Israelis with the purpose of wining back Palestine. Those who were driven out of their towns and homes already looked forward to going back home. Those groups began to attack the Israelis from the Jordanian lands. They would infiltrate the borders into their occupied land, attack the Israelis and run back to Jordan. The Israelis in turn would retaliate and bomb, with earth-to-earth missiles, the northern towns of Jordan. Irbid was often the target more than other cities. We would not know when such attacks would happen during the day or night. The Israelis terrorized the innocent civilians, including my family and I, day in and day out. As soon as we hear the first missile explode, we would run to the shelter. Many times we would get up in the middle of the night, upon hearing a missile explode, and run to the cold and damp shelter to spend the rest of the night there. My wife would always keep the most necessary things that we would need to take with us to the shelter handy in a basket by the door. In the winter, she always made sure that the children were dressed in heavy clothing with socks on as they lay in bed to go to sleep so that they are ready to get up and run to the shelter without delay.

This is ironic because I am reminded of when the children of Israel were ready to leave the land of Egypt the night of the Passover, Moses commanded "You shall eat the Passover with your loins girded, your sandals on your feet and your staff in your hand." Those children of Israel had to put up with that for only one night, while we had to live like that for a couple of years.

Black September

As my children grew out of the elementary school in Irbid, I requested to move to Amman so that my children could continue their education in our church school there. We rented a house near the airport, which was between Amman and Zarka. We chose this location so that my children could go to the school in Amman and, at the same time, I would be close to Zarka, where I was to minister.

When we first moved to Amman and lived near the airport, tensions grew between the Palestinian factions who united together to overthrow the King of Jordan and his Army. For a long period of time, which seemed like a year, street fights and shootings were happening almost everyday. Attempts to assassinate the King were happening often. The situation became dangerous.

During that time, the school in Amman was split into two shifts, morning for girls and afternoons for boys. I would drive our daughter Viola back and forth to school. Victor had to use public transportation on his own and come back home late at night. Most of the shootings and bombings would happen in the afternoons and continue into the late nights, much like what is happening in Iraq now in the year 2005. This was not a safe situation for Victor. He would come home terrified. At times, he would catch the last bus by miracle because when the shootings start, everyone runs and hides including the bus drivers. He was always afraid that he might not be able to make it home. He was scared many times as he watched people get shot and die on the bus in front of him. If we had lived closer to the school, he would not have needed to commute.

It was while we were living near the airport in 1970 that the Black September war broke out in Jordan. We lived in our shelter for 12 days under our house. There were 19 of us in the shelter including some of our neighbors. We cleaned and prepared the shelter one day before the war started. We stocked it with blankets, candles, food, fuel and water. Every one knew that we were about to have a war. Some people fled the country into neighboring countries where they had relatives or friends. Some went to Syria and many left the main cities to the countryside into their hometown villages.

On the second day of the war, more neighbors came asking to join us in our shelter. They were crying and terrified because their homes were bombed and they had to leave. We had enough room for the 25 of us. By now we could merely sit and stretch our legs from time to time. My wife used to prepare the food, we made sure the children were fed first. We had to economize and eat less since nobody could know when war would end. Our women would sneak out of the shelter to the house to bring food and, sometimes to bake bread. On many occasions, that bread would spoil and not be baked because bombs exploded nearby and they would turn off the oven and run back to the shelter.

In the shelter, we were closer to God and to Eternity as well. Those among the group who never prayed before had to have that desire now for protection. There was only one way out. It was heaven's intervention. We had no light to read our Bible. Light would expose us to shooting from either side. Non of the men among us could ever dare to get out of that shelter because of the danger of being mistaken for a fighter.

Oh God, save our country, stop the blood shed, let those in power come to their senses and have mercy for the children. From memory, we would recite passages that we could recall from Psalms 23rd, 91st, and 34th many times during the twelve days. No one could ever know anything about his next-door neighbors. We could only hear missiles and bombs exploding in the area. Out of the 15 houses in our neighborhood, our house was the only one left intact. That was one of the many miracles that God gave us. Not one of us was hurt. Tens of thousands were killed in that war.

On some occasions, a man would go out of his shelter to find a glass of water for his children and would never come back because he was shot to death.

Those who stayed with us and later left the shelter were astonished that our house stood unharmed. They said that it was because of us, being a family of God, that it was protected. In reality, it was an act of God's mercy. Before leaving our house to go down to the shelter, we opened our Bible and placed it on the table, knelt and asked God for protection. God, through his beloved son kept us alive and spared the house that we lived in. God's care and mercy will never be forgotten.

There was no more food for us in the house on the 11th day, near the end of the war. We heard over the radio that some food was sent from Lebanon to Jordan to help those in need. Practically, everyone was in need. The food stores in the area had very little left in them because people broke into them and took the foods that they found.

My wife, Victor and I, walked that day to the airport to see if we can get some food. We got a big bag of bread. There were lots people with the same idea and they were clamoring and fighting over the food that was being thrown at us from the airplane that had just landed from Beirut. As we were walking away with our bag of bread, one person who was not able to get any bread attacked us and took some of ours. We had very little bread as we got home.

Army trucks drove into our neighborhood the next morning and distributed flour, sugar and bread to the houses. Everyone could then come out of his shelter to enjoy daylight once more. All around looked like the day when God destroyed Sodom and Gomorrah, fearful and unpleasant. Though all were happy and thankful for having been spared to live again.

Saving The Orphanage and The School

During our stay in Amman, I was authorized to become the President of the Mission in Jordan. There were two problems to solve. Those were very important and difficult to handle.

The first problem was the Orphanage. The government's welfare department was not in favor of the mission's policy to not accept the number of orphans that it could accommodate. It could accommodate 50 orphans while those in charge would not allow more than 15. Our policy was to accept only Christians. In other words, our agenda was set up so that we could convert these orphans as well as their relatives to our church. It would be impossible to convert Moslems, as it was socially and politically unacceptable to do that.

Now, the orphanage was registered as a non-profit welfare project sponsored by the church. And since all such institutions, were regulated by the government, it was the responsibility of the government to insure that all institutions did well for the community regardless of race or religion. They are to be non-profit organizations with no discrimination whatsoever.

Being in authority now, it was my responsibility to solve this problem. The government threatened to nationalize the orphanage if the same policy continued. If it became nationalized, it would cease to be ours. Then all orphans would be admitted. The welfare department also demanded that any orphan should be preauthorized and admitted by them. They also demanded that religion should not be taught there otherwise, everyone should be taught his or her own religion. They also expected us to accept Moslems as well as Christians.

The church board was stuck. They thought to leave it in the hands of God and do nothing about it. The problem was serious. Our existence in Jordan was useless if we did not do good to the public. In fact, we would be suspected that our mission was to evangelize the Moslems, which is strictly forbidden.

As for the other Christian churches, we used to consider them non-Christians. They in turn, classified us as Jews following their old testament regarding keeping Saturday for a Sabbath.

Church members used to pray only. To solve the problem needed more than prayer. People in authority were concerned about the society's needs and looked for other help regardless of the sources. The country's resources were very limited in proportion to its needs. All organizations should not be self-centered. If the government, being a Moslem government, should care only for Moslems, what attitude would we have as Christians towards them?

On the other hand, God wants us not only to pray to him but also rather to do good to our fellow human beings. God would perform miracles only for those who are ready to help themselves. Those who do God's will, can help others with God's help.

Somebody told me one day of a group of women who prayed every time they met that God would send help somehow to a lady who was sick. That help never came to that home, because not one of those ladies who prayed ever volunteered to offer help be going her self and do the work for that lady. Prayer without action does not work.

Taking over those responsibilities was quite a challenge to me with that unpromising background. Of course, seeking God for wisdom and guidance comes first. Without him, I could do nothing. Going to the minister of welfare, I offered our services as good citizens of our country in any way that we can. He was very kind and understanding. He appreciated my offer and we began a good friendship. He said that he expected everybody to help. Then I was assured that his government had no intention to take the orphanage that we owned. At that time it was closed and sealed and the keys taken away. The only obstacle was the lack of communication between them and the former president of the mission.

As Christians, we are obligated to be concerned about other people's interests and try to help them. On the other hand, we can't expect others to cooperate with us if we are reluctant in offering help to them. If we are closed and can't see outside of our point of view, God will not be glorified through us.

We often boasted that we belonged to the right church. Our eyes and hearts are focused on our selves. We accumulate billions of dollars for fear of the unexpected while we do not want to show actual mercy outside our own circles. This is not Christ like. The world is looking for Christ through his real followers on earth.

My superiors in the church were stuck in the thinking that we should accept only Christians because it is legal to convert them in the future to our way of thinking. We could probably convert their families, thus increasing our membership. It is interesting that we had set up the orphanage as a non-profit organization while our hidden agenda was for profit, which is increased membership. I thought that this constituted hypocrisy.

I was troubled with these thoughts day and night. I could not rest until I could solve this problem and have the orphanage opened and run the correct way. I presented a solution to my superiors in the mission who in turn discussed my ideas and approved them. I was then able to accept Moslem orphans and provide a Moslem religion teacher to teach them their own religion. I was then in compliance with the welfare department and they allowed me the maximum number of orphans to house.

The second problem that I wanted to solve was the low enrolment of the Amman school. The tuition was very high and it was going up every year. The board members always increased the tuition every year because the budget was behind. So we were losing enrolment every year and the number of the students decreased every year. Our own church members started to send their own children to public schools because they were free. The board members did not care because they were able to get a discount for their own children's education. Also, The public schools never discriminated between Christians and Moslems. In other words, they showed better Christian spirit than us Christians.

Whenever any member sent his children to public school, we in the church used to look down upon them. They were classified as backsliders, as if they became non-believers. We would only pity them and pray for them. Those prayers were never heard or answered. Those simple hearted followers prayed for a long time that a way would be provided for the little ones to be able to receive education in their own church schools. Those prayers were never heard or answered as well. Who should hear and answer these prayers and how? Isn't it strange how many prayers go up to God and would be answered the right way. Who is involved in answering them, God alone, we, or both God and us?

As for those who are not of our own faith, if they could afford those fees, let them come, but not Moslems. We were afraid that they would find out that we were teaching their children our religion. They might protest. The government's role comes in to investigate and question the whole matter. Since they in their schools accept that Christians should be taught their own religion by one of their own. To be fair, we should accept Moslems and hire a Moslem teacher to teach their own religion to them. That was strongly opposed by the church committee. The same attitude was felt in Iraq when the government there asked all private and church schools to allow teaching the Koran and accept Moslems. Some Christian schools there accepted to comply with that order. Others refused to obey. Our own school in Baghdad, after we left Iraq, did not comply and was nationalized. This means that the government took it over. I alerted our committee that the same could happen in Jordan.

After being threatened several times, the Iraqi government took over the school in Baghdad to both manage and finance it. The government provided the school with teachers to teach their religion.

In the committee there was heated debate. Everyone wanted to prove that his idea to save the cause is the best. Some wondered why we should spend God's money on teaching the Koran instead of the Gospel. Some were afraid of the Moslems' influence over the school. This fear spread all over. That of course is lack of faith.

It took much effort and prayer on my part to persuade our own committee members in Amman. Later, a higher committee in Beirut was persuaded that that fear was groundless. I reasoned with them. First, if we stand on solid ground and know Jesus Christ real well, we should fear no consequences. Second, how could our institutions be evangelistic if we deny ourselves the privilege of serving others and at the same time deny them the privilege of joining us? Third, to start evangelistic activities, we should start with our own children who should be in their own schools. Not one of them should be missing regardless of money. Forth, the more Moslems are acquainted with their Koran, the closer they become to the Bible truth. Fifth, we should not be afraid to have good relations with the Moslems, if we lived our own faith as Christians. Sixth, the money we will spend on teaching the Koran is taken from the fees that they pay. We are spending a little of their own money to teach them their own religion. Seventh, the teacher who would teach that religion needs to be a Moslem, not a Christian. Eighth, the school fees should be reduced to make it possible for all who wish to join to be able to do so. Ninth, by reducing the fees we would have more students, more money to cover the expenses as well as teachers' salaries. Tenth, instead of having one teacher for 3 to 6 students, the classrooms can accommodate up to 20. Eleventh, the teacher would feel better having more children to teach because there would be more excitement and more life in the classroom. Twelfth, if we neglected to do that, we would not be Christians trying to apply the Christian love. We would lose our own children. We would lose the evangelistic touch and as a result lose the schools. That would lead to the church's starvation and death. I thought it was a shame that our school, which started many years ago should decline while other, newer schools in the area should prosper.

Such reasoning made the mission in that part of the world think twice about what should be done before it was too late. We had no time to lose. The golden opportunities would never come back before the time comes when we feel bad about ourselves.

They finally agreed that I work out my plans. We advertised that we were now open for everybody. Parents started to bring their children for registration and the number of students began to grow. Instead of having only 40 students, this year we had 150 to start. More money started coming and more life penetrated the school. The playground was full with all kind of different activities. A Moslem teacher was hired not only to teach the Koran, but also as a regular teacher. She proved to be better than some of our own teachers. The school became a success and it is still ours.

Mandatory Friday Law

During my ministry in Jordan rumors spread that the government wanted to enforce Friday as the weekend holiday. The Christians were very offended as they heard about the proposed new law. They were afraid that their day of worship would be done away with. That would be a first move toward persecuting Christians. Also, that meant as a step forward towards trying to convert them into the Moslem faith. Some Christians though did not care that much. To them, all the days were alike, since they were not practicing their religion.

Our church followers were the most offended. They were opposed to any laws that would take away their religious freedom. The most affluent members of our church came to me for counseling. They suggested many ideas, expecting the worst possible scenario to take place. We finally agreed that a written petition be signed and taken by hand to the Jordanian Prime Minister.

That was considered to be too daring a step to take. They were afraid, as a denomination that steps had already been taken towards enforcing the Friday law, similar to the expected Sunday law in the USA, where Sunday is the only observed day. Our fear was that we would eventually be forbidden to worship on Saturday, our day of worship.

A day was set for that meeting with the man in power. As we entered into his office, he was very kind and humble. Being the group's spokesmen, I had to start the conversation with the prime minister. I began "your Excellency, I, the president of the Adventist denomination in Jordan and these gentlemen with me, members of the Amman church and leading merchants and citizens, we consider it an honor and privilege to visit you at this time. We are proud of our country, government and His Majesty King Husain." He said, "you are very welcome, it is a privilege to have you. You are our men, we are proud of you. What can I do for you?"

"We heard some rumors, your Excellency, about issuing a decree that all businesses in Jordan should close on Friday. Such a law would affect our merchants who always closed their stores on Saturdays. If they close on both Friday and Saturday, it will result in a great financial loss for them. We keep Saturday out of religious conviction. If your Excellency sees fit for the good of the public and those employees who's day off is Friday, to allow our merchants to open their stores on Friday to make it possible for those people to do their shopping. This would give our people six days' work like the rest of the citizens, and we would be grateful and thankful."

The prime minister answered, "your point has been well explained and it is worthy of consideration. Yet, when we thought of issuing that decree, we had in mind to organize the country. It looks good to us to have all citizens have one day off. Everybody would enjoy it. You know the majority here are Moslems, we never intended to hurt anybody's feelings or livelihood. We did not intend to hurt you."

I said, "does this mean that our people can open their stores on Friday your Excellency?" He said, " cheer-up, be sure we will do all we can to make you happy. Your request will be studied and considered."

It was kindly considered and our merchants were allowed their request. Other Christian churches were waiting and watching. They planned, if we were successful in our approach, they too would apply for their Sunday and open on Friday. Later they applied and were granted their request.

You can see that it was fear that made people hesitant to ask for what they believed was right. It was fear that made Adam run away and hid. He was afraid because he sinned. Why fear if we are in the right?

Anecdotes, Places And Events

One sermon costs a suit

Present day religion is well illustrated in the following story. A minister got up one day to preach. It was an excellent sermon. He told his congregation that a Christian is a Christian only when he shows love and mercy to his fellow men. Your neighbor, he said is everyone. If you, therefore, had two suites and your brother or neighbor had non and he asks you for one, give him one of yours. Feed the hungry who come to you. Everyone present was delighted to hear that great sermon.

The minister's wife had to leave church early. She wanted to set the table for lunch. Her husband had to wait a little longer to greet the worshipers and shake hands with them. He also was glad to hear their comments and encouraging remarks. As the minister's wife was setting the table, the doorbell rang. As she opened, a beggar was there asking for help. He said I am a poor man. I am hungry and cold. I need some food and clothing please. You good people have mercy to a poor brother of yours. The woman responded. Oh yes, you are right. You are my husband's brother; my husband said it from the pulpit this morning. Come in, you blessed of the lord, feel at home.

She gave him food to eat and one of her husband's suites to keep him warm and happy. The man was grateful and went away praising the lord for that devoted woman who applied God's real love without hesitation.

The minister came home later for lunch and was happy to see that his wife had already set the table. He wanted to relax and change his priestly robe and put on one of his everyday suites before he ate his lunch. Having not found his favorite suite, he asked his wife about it.

116

She said, "well dear, your brother came in a short while ago, he was hungry and cold, so I gave him some food to eat and that suite to put on. You have other suites to wear."

"You crazy dear wife of mine, what I preach is for others, not for us."

Does this story sound familiar? How many people do not walk their talk?

Ninety days fever

My father was baptized in the year 1931 and joined the church. I was eleven years old. I took sick with a typhoid fever. My father, being a natural physician, practicing the old traditional medicine, tried all he could to save me. Two months went by with no success. The next thirty days, I was left alone to die in peace when my hour struck.

It was the later part of the year that two German pastors from the church came to visit us. Realizing that the family environment was sad, they asked if anything was wrong? "Yes" my father said, "my son Najeeb is sick for 90 days now."

"Have you given him any medicines?"

"Yes, but not for the last month."

"All medications failed and all endeavors proved nothing."

"Have you prayed for him, brother Naser?"

"Yes, I did, we did, but no response yet."

"Do you mind if we pray for him?"

"Of course, I would not mind, and I would be thankful if you did."

All I could remember was that both ministers and my father came over and surrounded my bed, knelt and prayed. I went to sleep and my sleep lasted 24 hours after which I got up, raised my head, and sat up in bed. Then I called my mother. She came running and was excited and astonished.

"Are you feeling well, my dear son?"

"Yes mother, I am very well. I want to get out to play with my friends."

She advised me to take it easy and did not allow me to go out on that day. I ate some yogurt then. The next day I felt even better and I was completely healed, thanks to my good lord and savior. He must have had a reason for sparing my life. I then made a covenant to proclaim his goodness and preach his Gospel.

Three one-eyed-sons

The following event is to be considered one of the outstanding miracle working powers of God.

One evening, I was giving a bible study to a group of people in my hometown of Al-Husn, Jordan. The study was about reaching heaven on a ladder. That ladder was meant to be prayer. It was such an interesting subject, that everyone present was affected.

A mention was made of the way and manner that we should approach God with our requests. When we ask the lord for anything, I said, we should make sure that we ask him for the best, because he has the best for his children. You would not tell him, "Lord I want the Best husband, but if that is not available, anyone will do, or, I want the best woman for a wife, and again if that is not possible, any woman will do." You really want the best, and the one that would last, don't you? God would give you the best and that might take some time until you are ready for the best. You have to be the best to get the best. A lady from the group could not take it any longer. She stood up and interrupted, saying "listen, you the son of Naser, what you say is right. If you do not mind, I'll have something to prove this."

"Ok", I said, "go on"

She started, "as I was married, I had no doubt that I would have children like any other woman around, but God gave me non. I began to ask him, as though he were to blame, to give me some children. Why should I be barren while other women are fertile? I argued with God, why should I be left to reproach? God did not answer me. One night, I went out of my room, faced the south, (she was a Moslem, and facing the south meant facing Mecca, where profit Mohammad's tomb stands). I put my hair down, tore off my dress, lifted up my hands towards heaven and said, oh God give me a boy even if he had only one eye." She said that she went back to her room and God answered her prayer and at delivery, it was a boy. "Do you know my first born son?" she asked?

"Of course I know him, he is my class-mate at school. His name is Khalaf."

"How many eyes does he have?"

I said, "only one"

"God gave me a second boy, do you know him?"

"Sure I do."

"How about his eyes?"

"Again, he is a one eyed boy and his name is Khlaif."

"God gave me the third boy, what do you know about him Azar?"

I said, "the third boy is also a one eyed boy, his name is Awad."

She said, "after the three boy gifts, God gave me a girl, what do you know about her eyes?"

I said, "She has two beautiful eyes."

"You see," she concluded, "if I had enough faith and courage to ask for a real good, healthy and sound boy, I would have been given all my boys perfect and without any defect."

Would it mean that we degrade God when we ask him for imperfect gifts, if he is our father and is also perfect, all wise, all powerful and the source of all good gifts. Why not come to him boldly and with faith and he will give us what we ask for. But we also should leave it to him to decide according to his will.

Death as an answer

There was a man who lived in Karak, Jordan, when I lived there. That man's mother got paralyzed for two years. As it is in every house, it gets boring when sickness tarries. When a member of a household suffers, all other members share that suffering. In that case, the whole family was sick.

That man could not watch his mother suffer that much for that long. His wife did all in her power to make it easier for her mother-in-law. She fed, cleaned, washed and powdered her all over everyday. Those services took most of her time. Anybody in that situation would be relieved for the least kindness shown to her by her family. We do not always expect much from our patients, because they need encouragement the most. Sometimes, they are nervous and their mood is bad. Those who are not in the same boat with them are expected to treat them with the most kindness and love.

That sick mother was that kind of nervous person. It added to the problems of her daughter-in-law, both physically and psychologically. Though, she never grumbled or complained. She would always give glory to the name of the lord. Isn't it great to serve your savior in the person of those tormented by affliction?

Though that good woman has been worn out as a result of her labor of love, burning like a candle in order to give light to those in need of it.

The old sick woman was expected to die any moment after those two years of suffering. She struggled, trembled and was fearful for a long time. She suffered for days and would not die. People, around her, thought that she lacked faith and trust. She needed confidence in order to die. They began thinking of somebody who would give her courage and their message came to me through her grand daughter.

"Pastor", she said, "you haven't visited us in a long time. Would you please come to us today, now?"

"Is there any urgent need for my visit now?"

"Yes, my grand mother is dying and my father sent me to ask you to come right away."

I went immediately, taking my bible with me. There, I found that room where that dying woman was, full of both relatives and friends. Everyone was so sad that their sick woman suffered that much for that long, hanging between life and death. "Please pastor", began her son, "would you read some texts from the Bible and pray for my mother." Would you for God's sake give her some confidence in Jesus, her savior."

Approaching the dying woman, I opened my Bible and read some promises for those who would take Jesus as their personal savior. I read also Psalm 23rd, which starts with "The Lord is my shepherd." I made sure that she heard every word. Then I knelt by her bed and prayed that God would grant her the assurance of forgiveness. After that I went home.

Upon reaching home, that man's same daughter who asked for my visit, came to tell me the good news, that her grand mother passed away moments after I left, and she conveyed to me her father's appreciation and thanks.

I never meant that the woman should die, nor would I ever do it for any sick or dying person. I am a strong believer that God could and would heal any disease if asked by faith. But there you are, that lady needed to rest and be relieved. Others were suffering for her sake. God's thoughts are never like ours. His ways are different from our ways.

Lost before and after conversion

Between 1944 and 1946 I was assigned to work in the Jerusalem district. I lived across the street from the King David Hotel in East Jerusalem. My visitation took me to the house where a relative of my mother lived with his family. I used to visit them on a regular basis from week to week. Usually, his wife was there by her self, her husband drove a taxi car and the children went to school. Her husband lived a very wild life cursing, putting his wife down, beating his children, drinking and smoking. His wife's only hope was that he comes back to his senses and act as a real loving husband and father. She told me that she went to church and always prayed for him. When he saw her reading her Bible, he would take the Bible and throw it away, cursing and using foul language. Later, though, her way of living and the love she showed him began to turn him around. He would ask her to take him with her to her church. She would not accept his offer because she was afraid he would act crazy or foolishly. She told him where the church was located. He went by himself several times until a change started to show on him. After that she agreed to accompany him to church. He got converted and became a different man. He would go to church and when he was at home, he would spend his time reading his Bible. He began to fast and eat limited amounts of unhealthy foods only once a day. His health began to become weaker and lost a lot of weight.

She also told me that he never sits at the table to eat with his family because he was devoting all his time for Jesus. She asked me to be kind enough to go to them when he was at home to talk to him. She also wanted me to eat with them hoping he would respect me and eat with us. She said, "you know, I was losing him when he lived the wicked way and I am losing him now after he was converted to Jesus Christ, what should I do now? Would you please help us?"

I began visiting that family when the husband was there. Sitting at the table with them for lunch. I invited him to join us. He did, because he wanted to show respect to me. While talking, I was stressing the beauty and importance of the husband sitting, eating and communicating with his family. He said that he did not eat more than once a day. When I asked him why, especially that he was not fat, he said he was in a big debt to Jesus that he wanted to fast for the rest of his life. Though I tried to convince him that Jesus did not require anything from him because he died for him and forgave him. No matter how hard I tried, I could never convince him, he would not be persuaded.

When he lived the loose wrong life, cussing and cursing, his passengers reported him to the owner of that taxi company who fired him and took him back later because he was the only source of income to support his family. When he was converted, he began preaching to every passenger. He became over-zealous and over-excited and wanted to force everybody to accept his savior. Again, the customers got offended and complained to his boss. At that point, he was fired for good.

That situation reminded me of an old time proverb recorded in Ecc 7:16-18 which reads, "do not be over-righteous neither be over-wise, why destroy yourself? Do not be over-wicked and do not be a fool, why die before your time? Avoid all extremes." Another old Arabian proverb says, if you chose to be too hard, you will be broken – if you be too lenient, you will be squeezed.

That man was on the extremes at both ends. It did not help him neither does it help anyone else. Many people follow that way of living. In fact, they would not help glorifying God because God never wants anybody to come to him out of fear.

So, I would say, take it easy on your self, be moderate in following your convictions. Don't hurt others with you Zeal. Be a moderate in what builds and helps you in eating and drinking. Abstain completely in whatever hurts you and offends those people whom you try to help. Give God the priority to workout his plan, his way. Be as good to others as God is good and patient to you.

Prohibited to enter the convent

In Jerusalem, in the Christian quarter, I rented a room in which we held our church services. And to reach to that room, you would have to walk from east Jerusalem through the Damascus Gate into old Jerusalem. Among our first converts, was Mary, an Armenian lady who was very faithful and devoted to her newfound faith? One day, she asked me to hold meetings in her home for those relatives and friends that she invited. The Terzibashian family, were among those invited. The truth of God's word became so precious to them that they wanted me to visit them in the Armenian Orthodox convent, where they lived. Prior to living in that convent, they lived in their own property outside the walls of Jerusalem. They had to run away as a result of the 1948 war between the Arabs and the Jews. So, they became refugees and their convent offered them monthly food rations, a house to live in, as well as other privileges. All of that was free. Anyone who was in need, regardless of race or religion, could get help by asking the convent. I should commend on the Catholics and the Orthodox for that.

I visited the Tarzebashians' home there from time to time. My wife accompanied me often. Jesus love found an access into their ready hearts. That was a family of a father, mother, three sons and two daughters. An exemplified a real loving and lovable Christian family. Christ's love, peace and Joy began to show on them. You can never light a candle and not expect it to shine.

Those repeated visits aroused prejudice and jealousy in those fanatic Armenian Church leaders. As a result, that family had to face opposition and threats if they decided to follow another faith, they would be denied all those privileges. They would no longer be eligible for those benefits. They would have to look for another house to live in, which would involve money for rent. They could not afford to lose all that, including the food they got.

It was a hard choice to make. They decided to be baptized to join the church they loved, which resulted in an order issued by the convent's authorities, that I should never be allowed to visit that convent. Death was waiting for me if I did. They threatened to kill me if I endeavored to enter the gate of the convent once more. They wanted to cut off that family from any communication with their new faith.

As Abraham, the second son of the Tarzibashians was laying on his back, reading his Bible, his mother interrupted, "Abraham, would you go up to the Mount of Olives and ask Pastor Azar about the exact time we should leave for baptism?"

"OK mom, I will go after finishing the chapter that I started to read."

"Ask him also, if it is OK to take lunch with us, it would be nice to spend the rest of the day by the Jordan River where our savior was baptized?"

"OK mom, I will do that too."

Abraham walked down those steps into the streets all the way to Damascus gate (called Bab-El-Amoud) and boarded a bus to take him to the Mount of Olives. That bus stopped at the corner, near our house and Abraham went down and started to cross the road. At that moment, a car loaded with four doctors going in that direction to the Augusta Victoria Hospital on top of the Mount of Olives, failed to stop and hit Abraham as he was crossing the road and broke his leg. Those doctors took him and treated him in that hospital.

Early next morning, Abraham's parents, came to us to tell us about that event. We felt bad about it. We thought that Satan attacks God's children whenever he can. He wanted to weaken this family's faith.

Right after Abraham had that accident, his parent's neighbors at the convent started to make fun of them. They told them that God was punishing them for changing their faith. As they were visiting us that morning, we asked them how they took that accident to mean? And what affect it had on their former decision to follow their Lord? The wife said, "While everybody blames us, we took it that Satan wanted to hinder us from walking with Jesus, we are still decided to be baptized."

It was a memorable day for that family as they joined their Lord and followed him. We had a great time together at the Jordan River.

As for Abraham, he too followed his Lord as soon as he got well. Later, his brother George joined the Middle East College to major in theology. He later served our mission in Iran. Abraham also went to the same college and later he met Sarah who was visiting in the Holy Land and thought that they should marry. After they got married they had a baby boy that they called Isaac. It is interesting how Abraham married Sarah and they had a baby son called Isaac. After Isaac, they had a baby girl they called Rebecca. Abraham and his family later came to the United States and completed his studies in California.

Dream becomes reality

This happened when we were in Basra Iraq. I knew the family and used to visit them. A telegram came one day to a doctor in Basra from his brother who lately graduated as an engineer in the USA. It said that he would land in Beirut, Lebanon, on a given date and time and asked his brother to meet him there.

The doctor went to Beirut and welcomed his brother. It was a great time for both of them. After spending some time in Beirut, the engineer suggested that they go up to the mountain to visit his fiancé before leaving for Iraq. They rented a car and headed towards the mountain. Another car was coming down that narrow road that they were on and both cars collided and both brothers were killed.

News came to Basra about that tragic accident which took away the life of that family's only two sons. Both parents, with their only daughter sat in utter shock and sadness. They were as still as stones. Tears continually ran down their faces mingled with sobs of anguish. There, people have the custom to go to a bereaved family's house as often as they could to console and comfort. In that case, however, no words could be found for comfort with both sons gone. It looked as though the light of that house had gone out. I happened to have gone to console them as well. Several days went by until one day an Armenian lady went into that house to comfort them. The lady sat for a few moments, she noticed that nobody said a word that would lighten his or her great burden. She thought she had some kind of consolation, so she started, "my dear friend would you stop crying for a few minutes until you hear my story?"

"Do you have a story worth hearing in our case?"

"Yes, I do," she said.

"Go on, "the bereaved mother said."

"After getting married, God gave me the first son. When he was two years old, he took sick and died shortly after that."

"Is that your story?" Interrupted the mother.

"This is not the story that I intended to tell you. But would you please listen until I come to it?"

"OK, Go on."

"After the death of my first child I had another, who again, when he got to be two years old, he got sick and died."

"You mean to tell me that you too, lost two sons like me, but they were still kids?"

"That is not my story."

"What is it lady."

"I had four of them, and they all died after reaching the same age."

"Oh, That is very sad"

"Now I will start telling you my story."

"You still have a story to tell after you lost four children like that?"

"God gave me the fifth son. That time I decided to take the best care of him after losing the other four. I thought that I shouldn't lose the fifth one."

"Yes, and do you have him still?"

"When my boy was about two years old, I neglected all house work and attended to him day and night, and one day"

"Got sick?" The bereaved mother interrupted.

"No, he did not. He was a healthy happy boy and I was having a great time playing with him. When time came that he should go to bed, I put him on my legs and rocked him to sleep."

"And then, what?"

"As I was doing that, instead of my son sleeping and because I was so tired, I slept before him. In my sleep, I had a dream. I saw my child grow up until he became a man. He was forming bad friendships, smoking, drinking and gambling. He would fight with people. One day, in my dream, a policeman knocked on my door, as I opened, he told me that my son has asked to see me. I asked him where my son was, and if anything happened to him? He informed me that he had been sentenced to death and wanted to see me before he died. That shocked me. And I cried out of fear. I opened my eyes and looked and found that my son was still in my lap, still a child two years old."

"Is that the end of your story, my friend?"

"No, as I looked at my son, he was pale. As I touched him he was cold and lifeless. As I put my hand over his mouth, there was no breath. He was dead."

"What did you do next?"

"I had no tears to shed. I was trembling all over. Then I took courage, lifted my son, put him on his bed and covered him as though he was sleeping."

"How did your husband take it?"

"Whenever my husband came back from work, he would first ask about our son. This time, all I could do is point him to the bed – there he is, he looked and thought the boy was sleeping. He asked to have his lunch as usual. His food was already placed on the table. He invited me to join him as usual I said that I already ate. That was a lie because I ate nothing. I wanted my husband to eat and have his desert before I told him about what happened. After he ate and I cleared the table, I asked him to sit down and hear me relate to him the dream I had. I came to the point where I found out that our son was dead. Then I told him, now my dear husband, control yourself and take it easy. As for me, I did not cry feeling that it was heaven's intervention. God made it possible for me to see in the dream that lovely child grow. He allowed me to watch what his destiny would have been if he grew up to be a man. God chose to save him from that terrible future. And who knows if all our children escaped similar destinies. I told my husband to get up, take our son, burry him, trusting the Lord, accepting his wisdom and will."

That was the best consoling story that family ever heard in their time of sorrow. They were greatly comforted.

The Church of the Holy Sepulcher

According to some traditions, The Church of the Holy Sepulcher inside the old city of Jerusalem was the place where our savior is supposed to have been crucified and buried. The big Building belongs to many denominations. It is entered into from one big wooden door leading to those many different churches with their different ways of worshiping. These churches were the Greek Orthodox, The Catholic, Byzantine Catholic, Assyrians, Copts and Armenian Catholics. All of these denominations used to be at war with each other to control the big wooden gate and the key to the gate. This is a traditional, long standing disagreement, which spanned the centuries. It was the Moslem Khalif, Omar El Khattab, who concurred Jerusalem in the Seventh Century AD, who resolved this long-standing problem by assigning the key to a prominent Moslem family. An assigned person from that family, the Nussiebeh family, is still keeping this key to this day. I took some visitors to the Holy Sepulcher to show them around and when we wanted to leave we found that we were trapped inside because the Nussiebeh Guard had to go to lunch, so he had to lock up the main gate for one hour, as was the agreed upon tradition. The gate was and still is locked for one hour every day.

Bethlehem

The Church of the Nativity in Bethlehem is the traditional spot where Jesus Christ was born. This too includes many Churches from different denominations as in the Church of the Holy Sepulcher. A very narrow and low door leads to the building with the churches inside. This is being taken to indicate that no matter how great a person might be, if he wants to come to God he would have to lower himself and put away his pride (read 1 Pet 5:5&6). I often volunteered to decorate the live Christmas tree in the court of the Nativity Church.

Many would sacrifice both time and money in order to be on the ground of the Church of the Nativity on the midnight of the Savior's birth, and to share that great celebration. Those who stayed at home would turn on their radio sets to hear Bethlehem's Christmas bells ring announcing the birth of the world's redeemer.

The Dome of the Rock

This is the place where the Biblical Isaac (Ishmael, according to the Koran) was offered as a sacrifice. This is when God tested Abraham's faith and when Abraham passed the test, God spared Isaac's life by providing an animal sacrifice instead. Now the Dome of the Rock belongs to the Moslems who also believe that Abraham is their Father. This site is sacred to both the Jews and the Moslems. The Dome of the Rock is the most noticeable structure in the old city with its 24 karat golden dome. We could see the Dome of the Rock from our apartment and we could see our apartment from the Dome of the Rock.

Beit Faji

This is where the donkey was found and brought to Jesus to ride on and enter Jerusalem as the triumphant King of the Jews. Many other historical and religious places are in the area. For example, the upper room, where the Savior celebrated the Passover with his disciples. The potters field where Judas hanged himself after betraying his master.

Bethany (now called Azaria)

This town is not far from Beit Faji and within five kilometers of Jerusalem is now part of Arab east Jerusalem. This is the city of Lazarus who was buried not far from where he lived. That cave is a witness to this day of the Lord's power to resurrect the dead. I remember visiting that cave the first time, when I stood in front of the tomb and read the chapter that tells the story of his resurrection. I felt the presence of the Lord and how real it is. As I was reading, I was living the event as Jesus called "Lazarus come forth". I always thanked the Lord for the opportunity that he gave me to live and witness in the Holy Land where his Son walked the earth.

Jericho

Traveling eastward from Bethany you come to Jericho. People still point to the tree that Zakkaious climbed in order to see his Savior as he passed on that road. Jericho is about fifteen miles to the east of Jerusalem. The Jordan river is near Jericho about another five miles to the east. Some people until today prefer to be baptized in the same traditional spot where Jesus Christ was baptized.

Anathouth

Now called Anata is four miles north of Jerusalem was the hometown of the Prophet Jeremiah. Bethel (now called Beiteen) is ten miles north of Jerusalem. Bethel was the place where Jacob had the vision of the ladder stretched between heaven and the earth, resembling hope and courage that God gives to those who believe in him.

The Pool of Bethesda is the place where Jesus healed the thirty eight year old sick man.

The Pool of Silowam speaks of that blind man who received back his sight by the command of that Great Healer, washing off the clay that Jesus put on his eyes in its waters.

The End of This Part of the Journey

I am now 85 years old. My dear girl, my wife who served with me all of those years, whom I loved and cherished and was so privileged just to be in the company of, is two years in God's presence now, and I still linger here on His earth, missing her beyond explanation and hoping not to disappoint Him with my remaining service.

I bid you goodbye for now and hope for you that you will live your life listening to God. His voice is not a bomb blast or a scream, not even a dulling roar, but rather an almost breath like quality of voice that is only perceptible when one will quiet his life and actually give God the opportunity to speak. I am blessed above all that He loves me. God loves you.

Najeeb N. Azar's Chronology

1931   At the age of eleven, he gave his first pledge to be a minister after having been sick with high fever for 90 days when Jesus appeared to him in a vision followed by a prayer after which he slept 25 hours to wake up and go out to play with his friends. From that time on, everybody would refer to him as pastor Najeeb.

1937   At the age of seventeen, he affirmed his pledge when he was baptized in the Sea of Galilee near Nazareth.

1938   He had three months training on preaching the Gospel in Amman, the capital of Jordan, by his church's pastor who was residing there. He was the pastor who baptized him.

1939   Went to college in Beirut, Lebanon to study theology to become a minister. He had to do Gardening to pay for his education.

1942   He graduated finishing the prescribed course in the Adventist College and started his ministry in his own hometown. He would light the kerocine lamp and carry it with him where ever he scheduled to have meetings at night. There was no electricity at that time. Two to three meetings were held each night. He would give the same sermon at all the meetings for that same day. Some people would follow him to hear that sermon more than once. Many got interested and joined the church.

1943   The church board at the denomination's head office sent to him and urgent cable telling him "Proceed Immediately to Karak." Whether they did not want him to harvest what he sowed or that they thought a successful man would be the best to start a new project and a new church. He did not know their intent. Next morning he left to Karak (Biblical Moab.) On his arrival, he started holding meetings.

1945   He was assigned to go to the west bank of the Jordan to live in Jerusalem across the street from the King David Hotel. He started visitation from one town to another to arouse interest with his fiery sermons that were appreciated from their young preacher. This is when young Pastor Azar met with Dr. Moses who proclaimed himself the messiah. Pastor Azar debunked him publicly.

1946   The second false messiah was debunked and saved by Pastor Azar. This was the year he worked on two of his art charts that he hopes to put on one of his books. One chart was on love, where it comes from and where it is supposed to go. The other one is about faith in a quiz like language. A beautiful Jewish girl in Jerusalem had a crush on him and wanted to have him interested in her as well. When she found out that he did not have the time for her, she said, "I suppose you are in love with your Jesus," and left him alone.

1947   There was a project to follow up with in Aramoun, Lebanon. There, he started a school with four students. There were only three persons who were considered church members. He lived in one of their houses. The school enrollment grew and he had to rent a two-room house to hold more than 40 students. The church work grew as well and many people were converted in that year.

1949   That was the year when instead of being rewarded for his accomplishments, he got fired from the ministry asking him to get a job outside the church. They hoped he would accept their proposal to marry a girl they chose for him, which he refused to do. Also, this is the year when he contacted the Brazilian Consulate to immigrate to Brazil. Help was promised and the Consol offered to pay the fees. Again, this was the year when he was asked by the citizens of Aitha in Lebanon to open a school for their children. This was the funny strange school mentioned in the pages of the book.

1950

It was the year when he accepted to join the church again. His own hometown was assigned for him to revive the church and reopen the school there. Because he was single, it was easy for him to move so often. It was this year that on his way from Lebanon to Jordan that he got arrested by the Syrian Government for his beliefs and interrogated.

1951 – 1954

These were the years when he started a very good and successful school. The church was revived with different programs and activities. The church members helped with those activities going to the villages around with the message. It was then that he met the Elaimy Family to send their son to the Middle East college and later his sister Najla. Najla spent almost two years when he started to think seriously of marrying her.

1954

Najeeb married Najla and lived in Karak where they started a successful school.

1955

Najeeb and Najla were blessed by having their first baby boy whom they called Victor.

1957

Viola was born which added to the happiness of the family. That year Najla stopped teaching so to take care of the children. Victor was two years old and Viola was 19 days old when another target was found to toss that family to. The Azars had to move to Ramallah in the west bank to be in charge of the Palestine district. They packed and moved. Before they even had the chance to unpack, they were ordered by the governor of Jerusalem to get out of the west bank and go back to Jordan. The details are in this book.

1958   The Azars were moved to Jerusalem and lived on the Mount of Olives. Their daughter Katy at 19 months dies and is buried there.

1960   A conference board vote stated the Azars should move from Jerusalem to Al-Husn where they said the work was not progressing. The Azars accepted the call and hoped this time they would settle down for at least five years. For the five expected years, they stayed there only five months. By the end of that year, they were called to go to Beirut where he was ordained to the ministry with his wife standing by his side. Taking advantage of the ordination, they proposed that they should be moved to Basra, Iraq, to revive the work there and build a church. Najeeb's wife agreed to the proposal and they moved to Basra.

1961   Their daughter Katy was born taking the same name of the Katy that died in Jerusalem. That year Najeeb's Mother passed away as they were unpacking in Basra. That was a great loss for them. After spending a few months in Basra, they were moved to Baghdad to lead that church.

1962   Visiting the Baghdad Church, the president of the division came to visit Baghdad and was astonished to find out that the Azars were in Baghdad and ordered the Azars back to Basra. During the stay in Baghdad, they witnessed the first revolution or civil war in Iraq.

1963   While living in Basra, the Azars witnessed the second revolution or civil war when the Baath party took power.

1964   A beautiful church was built in Basra under the direction of pastor Azar.

1966   Samir was born and the third revolution broke after the assassination of President Abdul Salam Aref.

1967   The Azars were recalled to Jordan to serve in their hometown. The move happened during the six-day war between the Arabs and the Jews. Pastor Azar was coming into Jordan with the family belongings in the truck along side the Iraqi army as they crossed into Jordan to help with the war effort.

1967   Lived in Irbid, Jordan, for the next two years under the constant threat and bombing of the Israelis. The Azars always had to run to the shelter when Israel attacked at night.

1968   The Azars were moved again by the church to live in Amman where Pastor Azar rescued the church orphanage and school from closure or nationalization by the government.

1970   They witnessed rising tensions between the PLO and the Jordanian army that resulted in the terrifying war of Black September. That was the year when they decided to immigrate to America.

1971   Pastor Azar was promoted to be the president of the Jordan mission.

1973   The Azars immigrated to the United States where the dream of freedom was fulfilled.

About the Author

Pastor Najeeb Azar is a retired Christian minister who served and preached in many Middle Eastern countries. He is responsible for establishing many schools, churches and an orphanage in the Middle East. He is widely published and respected as an authority on the similarities between Christianity and Islam. His articles were published in many newspapers and magazines in the Middle East. When he and his family came to the USA, he became a businessman and helped his children start very successful businesses.

Printed in the United States
52172LVS00005B/205-357